THE
NEW RETIREE'S KICKSTART GUIDE

THE ULTIMATE FUNNY RETIREMENT GIFT!

IMPRESSUM

© **2024 TG Edition**

1st edition

Author: Isabella Greenfield

Design: Julia Kofler

Image reference: Freepik

ISBN: 9791281216655

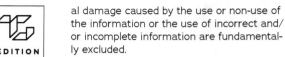

CONTACT

TG Edition

Thomas Larch

Feldbauernweg 22

39010 St. Martin in Passeier

Italy

E-Mail: support@tg-edition.com

DISCLAIMER

COPYRIGHT

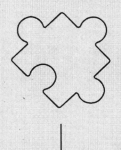

UNLOCK YOUR
FREE PUZZLE
COLLECTION!

Get access to our
free collection
of *Sudoku, word searches,*
and *crosswords*

—perfect for keeping your brain sharp and
having some fun at the same time. Whether
you love a quick puzzle in the morning or a
relaxing word search to wind down, there's
something for everyone.

SIMPLY **SCAN THE QR-CODE**, DOWNLOAD YOUR PUZZLES AND START SOLVING RIGHT AWAY!

CONTENT

HOW I SURVIVED RETIREMENT (AND YOU CAN TOO!) — **11**

Let me tell you a little story................ **12**

**CHAPTER ONE
WELCOME TO RETIREMENT!** — **13**

Now What?.................... **14**

From 9-to-5 to Cloud Nine............ **16**

Creating Your Dream Routine **18**

Activities to Enrich Your Retirement........... **20**

1. Settling into Retirement.............. **21**
2. Celebrating with Retirement Parties ... **23**
3. Reconnect with Family and Friends....... **24**
4. Creating a Bucket List............. **26**
5. Making a Vision Board............. **27**
6. Establishing New Routines............. **29**
7. Taking a Class............. **34**
8. Plan Your Travels............. **35**
9. Make Your Health Priority #1............ **36**

The Best is Yet to Come............ **38**

**CHAPTER TWO
FINDING MY PURPOSE** — **39**

Who Am I Without My Job?............ **40**

Who Am I Now?............ **42**

Activities for Uncovering Your Purpose **44**
1. Find a Purpose **45**
2. Discover and Pursue New Hobbies **48**
3. Join or Form a Hobby Group **50**
4. Set New Challenges **52**
5. Do Something New Every Day **54**
6. Set Personal Goals **56**
7. Continue Learning and
Share Knowledge **59**
8. Adopt a Growth Mindset **61**
9. Learn New Things **63**
10. Share Your Journey **65**

**Embracing Your New
Identity and Purpose** **67**
Suggested Reading List **70**

CHAPTER THREE
BOREDOM BUSTERS

73

Fun at Home **74**
Boredom Tips and Strategies **77**
**Exciting Activities for Your
Retirement Adventure** **79**
1. Gaming **80**
2. Gardening **82**
3. Be Creative **84**
4. Drawing and Painting **87**
5. Start a Blog or YouTube Channel **89**
6. Go on Adventures **90**
7. Woodwork/Handcrafting **92**
8. Photography **94**
9. Starting a Business **97**
10. Cooking and Baking **100**

Making the Most of Your Time at Home **103**

CHAPTER FOUR
HEALTHCARE HIJINKS
105

Navigating the Medical Maze 106

Understanding Your Healthcare Options107

Activities for a Healthy Lifestyle 110

    1. Healthy Eating **112**

    2. Healthy Cooking **113**

    3. Finding the Sport That Suits You **115**

    4. Exercising **117**

    5. Joining Fitness Classes **119**

    6. Group Sports **120**

    7. Lifting Weights **121**

    8. Creating a Training Plan **122**

    9. Daily Walk **123**

Healthy, Happy, and Thriving **124**

CHAPTER FIVE
MENTAL GYMNASTICS
126

Keeping Your Brain Active **127**

**Why Mental Stimulation
is Important in Retirement** **128**

**Tips and Strategies to Boost
Your Mental Fitness** **131**

Activities for Keeping Your Brain Active 134

    1. Train Your Mind with Apps **135**

    2. Mind Training with
    Games and Exercises **136**

    3. Reading **137**

    4. Writing a Book **138**

5. Research Your Family Tree **140**
6. Explore Creative Arts **142**
7. Discover New Skills **143**
8. Embrace Technology **144**
9. Dive into New Knowledge **146**
10. Meditation **147**

Curiosity Never Retires! **148**

CHAPTER SIX
SOCIAL SHENANIGANS

150

Staying Connected **151**
The Importance of Social Connections **153**
Practical Tips and Strategies **156**
Social Adventures **160**
1. Stay in Touch with Friends **161**
2. Keep in Touch with
Former Colleagues **162**
3. Make New Friends **163**
4. Spend Time with Family **164**
5. Get a New Pet **165**
6. Teach Others **166**
7. Get a Part-Time Job **167**
8. Online Courses **168**
9. Book Club **169**
10. Pet Sitting **170**

**Embracing Social Connections
in Retirement** **171**

CHAPTER SEVEN
TWO'S COMPANY
173

Balancing Love, Life, and Personal Space 174

The Importance of Communication 176

Compromise and Flexibility 178

Strengthening the Bond 180

Setting Joint Goals 181

Communication Tools 182

The Retired Couple's Playbook 183

    1. Date Nights with a Twist 184

    2. Nurturing Relationships
    in Special Ways 185

    3. Finding Shared Hobbies 186

    4. Cooking Together 187

    5. Traveling Together 188

    6. Attending Classes Together 189

    7. Game Nights 190

    8. Movie Night 191

    9. Conversation Starter Questions 192

    10. Volunteering Together 193

**Growing Together with
Love and Laughter** 194

CHAPTER EIGHT
MONEY MATTERS
196

Surviving Without a Paycheck 197

**Why Planning Is Your
Financial Superpower** 198

Practical Tips and Strategies 199

Activities: Making Money Management Fun................**202**

    1. Financial Check-Up................**203**

    2. Get Your Ducks in a Row................**204**

    3. Savings with a Smile................**206**

    4. Invest in Your Future................**207**

    5. Budgeting Fun................**209**

    6. Financial Confessions................**211**

    7. Frugal but Fabulous................**212**

    8. Deal Detective................**214**

    9. Zero-Dollar Entertainment................**216**

    10. Thrifty Travels................**218**

    11. Think Outside the Box................**220**

Financial Freedom With a Smile................**221**

CHAPTER NINE
GRAND ADVENTURE

223

Travel and Exploration................**224**

The Benefits of Travel and Exploration in Retirement................**225**

Practical Tips and Strategies................**228**

Activities: Making Travel and Exploration Your New Hobby................**232**

    1. Plan Your Next Great Escape................**233**

    2. Travel Your Own Backyard................**234**

    3. Explore Nature................**235**

    4. Hit the Trails................**237**

    5. Relive Your Youth................**239**

    6. A New Home Base................**241**

    7. Affordable Adventures................**242**

    8. Cultural Immersion................**245**

    9. Travel Buddies................**246**

    10. Travel with a Purpose................**248**

Adventure Awaits................**249**

CHAPTER TEN
GIVING BACK
251

Volunteering and Community Involvement...........252

Enriching Your Life Through Volunteering...........253

The Ripple Effect...........254

Finding Purpose and Fulfillment...........255

Overcoming Your Fears...........256

Practical Tips to Make Volunteering a Fun Adventure...........257

Exciting Ways to Give Back!...........259

    1. Volunteer in Your Community...........260

    2. Mentoring...........261

    3. Babysitting...........262

    4. Take Care of Your Grandchildren...........263

    5. Declutter and Donate...........264

    6. Support Charitable Projects...........265

    7. Neighborhood Initiatives...........266

    8. Host a Charity Event...........267

    9. Become a Pen Pal to Those in Need...268

    10. Advocacy and Activism...........269

The Power of Giving Back...........270

CHEERS TO RETIREMENT
YOUR NEXT GREAT JOURNEY
272

Congratulations!...........273

HOW I SURVIVED RETIREMENT (AND YOU CAN TOO!)

So, you've finally made it to retirement! You've punched the clock for the last time, trading in those Monday morning blues for, well, any shade of blue you want (personally, I prefer the blue of a clear sky and ocean waves). Now you're staring at the wide-open road ahead, wondering what in the world you're going to do with all this time. Trust me, I've been there, and that's exactly why I decided to write this book.

Let me tell you a little story

When I first retired, I had this grand plan. I was going to take up gardening. Simple, right? How hard could it be to grow a few tomatoes? Well, let's just say that by the time I was done, I had managed to grow precisely one tomato, which, judging by its size, had clearly been on a diet. But that's not the worst part. The worst part was when I decided to "impress" my neighbors with my green thumb, only to have them politely ask if I'd been planting pebbles instead of seeds. Yes, folks, it was that bad.

After that debacle, I knew I needed a new plan. Retirement was supposed to be fun, fulfilling, and full of new adventures, not just a series of failed attempts at hobbies that left me feeling like I was back in kindergarten. So, I did what any rational person would do: I started exploring all the things that could bring joy, meaning, and a good belly laugh into this new chapter of life. I dabbled in volunteering, took a stab at traveling (with much more success than gardening, I might add), and even dipped my toes into the mysterious world of budgeting—yes, you heard me right, budgeting!

And that's how this book was born. It's a collection of all the things I've tried, learned, and sometimes failed at, all wrapped up in a package meant to make you laugh as much as it makes you think. If I can spare you from a tomato-sized disappointment or help you find your new favorite hobby, then I'll consider this book a success.

So, grab a comfy chair, maybe a cup of something warm (or something stronger if that's your style), and let's dive into this crazy, wonderful journey called retirement.

Trust me,
it's going to be a blast!

CHAPTER ONE

WELCOME TO RETIREMENT!

Now What?

Congratulations! You've made it to the promised land of retirement, where every day is Saturday, and pants are optional until noon (or forever if you prefer). You've traded in the hustle and bustle of the 9-to-5 grind for the leisurely strolls of a new, exciting chapter in your life. So, grab your favorite beverage—whether it's a cup of coffee, a glass of wine, or a refreshing lemonade—and let's dive into the amazing journey of retirement together.

> **Retirement isn't an end;
> it's a glorious new beginning.**

Think of it as the longest, most enjoyable coffee break you've ever had. It's your chance to rediscover hobbies, take up new interests, and finally tackle that bucket list you've been compiling since disco was king.

Picture this:
You no longer hit the snooze button five times before dragging yourself out of bed.

Instead, you wake up when you want, ready to seize the day - whether that means a round of golf, a pottery class, or simply enjoying a leisurely breakfast without a single email to worry about. Remember that time when your colleague Jeff retired and started baking bread? He didn't just make bread - he made award-winning sourdough with the whole neighborhood knocking on his door. Jeff found his passion in the dough; now, it's your turn to find yours.

Of course, the transition can feel a bit like stepping off a speeding treadmill onto a serene beach. There's a brief moment of disorientation, but trust us, the sand between your toes feels fantastic!

So, welcome to retirement!
Let's set out on this exciting adventure
with a smile on our faces
and a spring in our step.

Here's to making every day count, discovering new passions, and enjoying the ride. Cheers to you and this incredible new phase of life!

From 9-to-5 to Cloud Nine

Embracing the Changes and Challenges of Retirement

Welcome to the wonderful world of retirement! It's like walking into a magical land where alarm clocks are a thing of the past, and your only meetings are with your morning cup of coffee. But as with any grand adventure, this transition comes with its own set of changes and challenges. Don't worry, though - we're here to make our way through this new terrain together, with plenty of laughter and joy along the way.

First, let's talk about the transition from work to retirement.

Imagine you've been driving at top speed on a highway for decades, and now you're suddenly cruising down a scenic country road. It's peaceful and beautiful, but it takes a moment to let your foot off the gas and adjust to the slower pace. You might find yourself reaching for your work phone out of habit, only to remember that the only emails you get now are about exciting travel deals and local yoga classes. It's a shift, but it is one filled with endless possibilities. Emotionally and psychologically, retirement is like the ultimate plot twist in the movie of your life. You've been the hardworking protagonist for so long, and now it's time to embrace a new role - the joyful adventurer. There might be moments when you miss the camaraderie of colleagues or the thrill of a deadline, but this is also an opportunity to rediscover yourself. Think of it as a second adolescence - minus the awkward braces and annoying curfews. You get to explore who you are without the constraints of a job description.

Daily life and routines undergo a delightful transformation, too. Gone are the rigid schedules and back-to-back meetings. Now, your calendar is a blank canvas, waiting for you to fill it with activities that bring you joy. Whether it's a morning walk, afternoon tea with friends, or an evening of stargazing, you can decide how to spend your time. It's like being handed the keys to your dream life, where every day is a chance to do something remarkable.

For example, take Uncle Joe, who spent 40 years as an accountant. On his first day of retirement, he woke up at 6 AM out of sheer habit, only to realize he had nowhere to be. So, he decided to head outside and start a garden. A year later, his tomatoes are the talk of the town, and he's never been happier. Retirement allowed him to nurture a passion he never had time for before.

Of course, there will be adjustments. You might initially feel like a ship without a compass, but soon, you'll find your direction. Embrace the changes, laugh at the little hiccups, and remember that this is your time to shine. Retirement is your reward for all those years of hard work. It's a new chapter filled with endless adventures, and you're the star of the show. So, get ready to enjoy every moment.

Trust us,
this is just the beginning!

Creating Your Dream Routine
Finding Joy in Everyday Retirement

You have now entered the land of endless Saturdays, where the only rush hour is the line at your favorite coffee shop. But even in this paradise of leisure, routines play a magical role in keeping life balanced, fulfilling, and fun. Let's look at why routines are the unsung heroes of retirement and how you can create your own perfect daily rhythm.

Routines structure daily life in retirement, transforming your days from a blank canvas into a masterpiece.

They provide a gentle framework that helps you make the most of your time, ensuring you can savor every moment without feeling adrift. Remember how you used to schedule meetings and deadlines? Now, you get to pencil in activities that make your heart sing - whether it's a morning stretch, a midday stroll, or a new and exciting hobby.

Creating new routines can be as exciting as discovering a hidden talent. Start by thinking about what brings you joy. Love gardening? Make it a morning ritual to tend to your plants while sipping your coffee. Enjoy reading? Dedicate a cozy afternoon nook where you can dive into a good book. The key is to blend activities you love with new ones you've always wanted to try.

Balancing leisure and responsibilities is the secret to a happy retirement.

Sure, you have more freedom now, but sprinkling in a bit of structure is still important. Think of it as the deliciously perfect mix of chocolate and peanut butter. Schedule fun activities alongside necessary chores, like doing laundry on Mondays, so the rest of the week is wide open for adventures.

And don't forget to pencil in some „*me-time*" for relaxation and self-care.

Reflecting on your personal interests and values is a beautiful way to create routines that resonate with your soul.

Take a moment to think about what truly matters to you. Are you passionate about staying fit? Block out time for yoga or a walk in the park. Love learning? Sign up for an online course or join a book club. Your routines should reflect your unique personality and passions, making every day an opportunity to celebrate who you are.
Take my neighbor, Betty, for example. She starts her day with a sunrise walk, spends her afternoons painting, and ends her evenings with a cup of tea and a crossword puzzle. Her routine is a beautiful blend of activity and relaxation, but most importantly, it is perfectly tailored to her interests.

ACTIVITIES TO ENRICH YOUR RETIREMENT

Retirement opens the door to a world brimming with fun, excitement, and discovery! Every day is a blank canvas, ready to be painted with the activities that bring you joy and fulfillment. Celebrate with loved ones, look into new hobbies, or set ambitious goals - this is your time to embrace the thrill of new beginnings. Get ready to explore, create, and live life to the fullest, turning your retirement into the most exhilarating chapter yet!

1. Settling into Retirement

So, you've clocked out for the last time, tossed your work shoes into the back of the closet, and are now facing the glorious horizon of retirement. To help you ease into this wonderful new phase, let's start with a few exercises for your mind and body.

First, let's tackle the mental transition.

One of the best ways to steady yourself is by setting aside a few minutes each day for mindfulness or meditation. It's easier than you think and incredibly effective at clearing your mind and teaching you to focus on the present.

Start by finding a quiet spot where you won't be disturbed. Sit comfortably, close your eyes, and take a few deep breaths.

Focus on your breathing
- in and out.

If your mind starts to wander (and it will), gently bring it back to your breath. Start with five minutes daily and gradually increase as you feel more comfortable.

There are plenty of apps to guide you through simple meditation practices. „Headspace" and „Calm" are popular options. They offer guided sessions that range from just a few minutes to longer, more in-depth practices. Insight Timer is another great app featuring a huge library of free meditations and soothing music.

Meditation helps reduce stress, improve focus, and boost overall well-being. Trust me, a little „om" goes a long way. Plus, it's a fantastic way to start or end your day calmly and positively.

Next, consider starting a journal.

Jot down your thoughts, dreams, and even those quirky ideas you've had on the back burner. Writing can be incredibly therapeutic and is a great way to process this significant life change. Plus, future-you will love looking back at these musings.

Now, for the physical side of things.

Start your day with some gentle stretching or yoga. You don't need to twist yourself into a pretzel; just a few easy stretches to get the blood flowing and keep those joints happy. And don't forget to get outside!

A *brisk walk* in the fresh air can do wonders for your mood and energy levels.

Try incorporating small moments of peace into your day for relaxation and awareness. Brew a cup of your favorite tea, sit in your garden, and just enjoy the moment. Listen to the birds, feel the breeze, and let yourself unwind. These small practices can make a big difference in how smoothly you settle into retirement.

2. Celebrating with Retirement Parties

It's time to party like it's 1999 - or whatever year you had the most fun. Throwing a retirement party is the perfect way to mark this exciting milestone and celebrate with the people who matter most.

Let's start with some party ideas.

How about a themed bash? You could go retro with a '70s disco night, complete with bell-bottoms and funky tunes. Or, if you're more of a beach bum at heart, a tropical luau with leis, tiki torches, and plenty of pineapple cocktails could be a blast. Don't forget the photo booth with fun props. Everyone loves a good laugh and a silly photo to remember the day.

A cozy backyard barbecue might be just the ticket if you prefer something more low-key. Fire up the grill, lay out some comfy seating, and let the good times roll. You could even have a potluck where guests bring their favorite dish. This eases the hosting load and adds a personal touch to the feast.

Celebrating with friends and family is essential. These are the folks who have cheered you on through thick and thin, and they deserve to share in your joy. Plus, a retirement party is a great way to reconnect and reminisce about the good old days while looking forward to the adventures ahead.

Remember, this is *your time to shine.*

Whether you go all out with a big bash or keep it intimate with a small gathering, the key is to have fun and make memories. So, gather your loved ones and crank up the music!

3. Reconnect with Family and Friends

Retirement isn't just about exploring new hobbies and ticking off bucket list items - it's also the perfect time to reconnect with family and friends. During our busy working years, these relationships can sometimes take a back seat, but now you have the time to reignite those important bonds.

First, let's talk about family.

Remember those times you promised to visit more often but ended up swamped with work? Now's your chance to make good on those promises. Plan regular visits or even spontaneous drop-ins to see your children and grandchildren. If you live far away, schedule regular video calls - technology can be a wonderful bridge.
Organize a family reunion or a fun weekend getaway. These events create lasting memories and give everyone a chance to catch up. Imagine a cozy cabin trip where you can play board games, go hiking, and share stories by the campfire. My friend Bob retired last year and decided to host a monthly "Grandkids Day." Each month, he plans a fun activity like treasure hunts in the backyard, baking cookies, or even building a birdhouse. The kids love it, and Bob is now the coolest grandpa around!

Now, let's not forget about friends.

Those lunch dates and catch-ups that were often postponed can now be a regular part of your schedule. Reconnect with old friends and make new ones by joining clubs or groups that interest you. Start a monthly potluck dinner with your friends. Each person brings their favorite dish, and you all get to enjoy a feast while sharing stories and laughs. It's a fantastic way to stay connected and enjoy good company. Remember Jessica from accounting? She started a book club with a twist - they read the book, watch the movie adaptation, and then discuss which was better. The group's lively debates and hilarious critiques have made it the highlight of her month.

Finally, consider creating new traditions with both family and friends.

It could be anything from an annual holiday gathering to a weekly game night. These traditions become cherished rituals that everyone looks forward to.

Reconnecting with the important people in your life adds richness and joy to your retirement. So, take the time to grow and nurture these relationships. Share your wisdom, listen to their stories, and create new memories together.

After all, the best part
of retirement
is enjoying it
with the ones you love.

4. Creating a Bucket List

Retirement is your golden ticket to dive into all those adventures you've dreamed about, and there's no better way to start than by creating a bucket list. Grab a pen and some colorful markers, and let's make this list as exciting as your newfound freedom!

First, don't hold back —write down everything you've ever wanted to do.

Always wanted to skydive? Put it on the list! Dreamed of learning to play the ukulele? Add it! This is your chance to think big and bold. Your bucket list should be a reflection of your wildest dreams and your most whimsical fancies.

How about taking a cooking class in Italy? Or training for a marathon? Maybe you've always wanted to start a beekeeping hobby or volunteer at a wildlife sanctuary. The sky's the limit, and retirement is the perfect time to explore these unique interests. Remember, it's not just about crossing items off a list - it's about the joy and fulfillment you'll find along the way.

Consider adding some „just because" activities that are purely for fun. Host a giant family reunion picnic, complete with three-legged races and watermelon-eating contests. Plan a road trip to visit all the quirky roadside attractions you can find, like the world's largest ball of twine. Or, aim to read one book from every genre, even the ones you've never tried.

Creating a bucket list is about *dreaming big* and *embracing the excitement* of what's to come.

So, go ahead and jot down those desires, no matter how weird or ambitious they may seem.

5. Making a Vision Board

Creating a vision board is like making a visual roadmap to your dreams, and it's a great way to get excited about your retirement goals.

Ready to get started?

Grab some magazines, scissors, glue, and a big piece of poster board, and let's turn those dreams into pictures!
First, gather your supplies. You'll need old magazines, printed photos, inspirational quotes, and anything else that catches your eye. Don't forget the essentials: a glue stick, scissors, and some colorful markers.

Now, find a comfy spot to spread out

01 COLLECT

Flip through those magazines and cut out images and words that resonate with you. Think about what you want to achieve, where you want to go, and how you want to feel. Whether it's a serene beach, a vibrant garden, or a bold phrase like „Adventure Awaits," if it sparks joy, it belongs on your board.

ARRANGE 02

Arrange your cutouts on the poster board. There's no right or wrong way to do this - just go with what feels right. You might create sections for different areas of your life, like travel, hobbies, health, and relationships. Or, you might prefer a more freestyle approach. Once you're happy with the layout, start gluing everything down.

03 PERSONALIZE

Add some personal touches. Write down specific goals, doodle little embellishments, or even sprinkle some glitter if you feel extra festive. This board is all about you, so make it uniquely yours.

and get creative. The benefits of a vision board are *magical*.

You're setting a clear intention for your future by visualizing your dreams and goals. It keeps you motivated and focused, reminding you daily of the wonderful things you're working toward. Plus, it's a fantastic way to stay positive and excited about what's yet to come. So, hang your vision board somewhere you'll see it often. Let it be a constant source of inspiration and a reminder that your retirement years are a time for growth, joy, and endless possibilities.

6. Establishing New Routines

Retirement means trading your work schedule for a life where you call the shots. While the freedom is exhilarating, creating new routines can keep your days fulfilling, fun, and organized.

Here's a *step-by-step guide* to help you establish routines that bring purpose and joy.

UNDERSTAND THE IMPORTANCE OF ROUTINES

First off, science tells us that routines are one of the secrets to a happy, healthy life. They provide structure, which helps reduce stress and improve mental well-being. With a routine, you wake up knowing what your day holds, making it easier to stay motivated and productive. Plus, routines can boost your brain power, helping to keep your memory sharp and your mind engaged.

02

CREATE A MORNING RITUAL

Start your day with a morning ritual that sets a positive tone. Here's how:

Wake Up at a Consistent Time

Try to wake up at the same time each day to regulate your body's internal clock.

Stretch and Move

Begin with some gentle stretching or a short walk around the block. This gets the blood flowing and energizes your body.

Healthy Breakfast

Enjoy a hearty breakfast while reading the paper or watching the sunrise. Consider including foods like oatmeal, fruits, and eggs for a nutritious start and energy boost.

Mindfulness

Spend a few minutes practicing mindfulness or meditation. Apps like Headspace or Calm can guide you through this.

03

SCHEDULE JOYFUL ACTIVITIES

Next, add activities you love.
This keeps your day purposeful and enjoyable.
Here's how to incorporate them:

Hobbies

Dedicate time to hobbies like gardening, painting, or learning to play a new instrument. Schedule these activities to ensure you make time for them.

Exercise

Include low-impact exercises such as yoga, swimming, or cycling. These activities keep you fit and healthy.

Social Time

Plan regular coffee dates with friends or join a weekly book club. This keeps your social calendar buzzing and maintains important social connections.

04

ESTABLISH AN EVENING ROUTINE

Wind down with an evening routine to signal your body that it's time to relax. Here's a simple plan:

Quiet Hour

Spend the last hour of your day away from screens. Read a book, listen to calming music, or try some light stretching.

Journaling

Reflect on your day by journaling. Write about what you enjoyed, what you're grateful for, and any plans for tomorrow.

Relaxation

Enjoy a soothing cup of chamomile tea before bed. This can help you unwind and prepare for a restful night's sleep.

05

STICK TO YOUR ROUTINES

Consistency is key. Stick to your routines as much as possible, but also allow flexibility for spontaneous fun. This balance keeps your days structured yet exciting.

By establishing new routines, you create a balanced, purposeful retirement that's both relaxing and exciting. It's all about finding what makes you happy and weaving it into your daily life.

7. Taking a Class

Retirement is the perfect time to embrace the joy of learning something new. Engaging in structured learning can keep your mind sharp, introduce you to new friends, and add excitement to your days. Plus, it's a fun way to explore interests you never had time for before.

There are countless benefits to taking a class. Studies show continuous learning can improve memory, boost mental agility, and even enhance emotional well-being. Plus, it's a great way to stay socially active and meet like-minded folks who share your interests.

So, what kind of classes should you consider? The possibilities are endless! You could explore your artistic side with painting, pottery, or photography. If you're a nature lover, why not try foraging? Learn how to identify edible plants and mushrooms, and discover the hidden culinary treasures in your local woods.

Feeling adventurous? Give paddleboarding or sailing a go.

Not only will you learn a new skill, but you'll also enjoy some fantastic outdoor exercise. Consider a cooking class if you've always been curious about the culinary arts. From mastering the basics to exploring gourmet cuisine, there's something for every level of expertise.

When it comes to finding these classes, start by checking out your local community centers or colleges. Many offer a wide range of courses, from night classes to weekend workshops. Libraries often host free or low-cost classes, too. Don't overlook online platforms like Coursera, Udemy, or MasterClass, where you can learn everything from coding to creative writing at your own pace.

Look for niche courses like cheese-making, beekeeping, or even acting for something truly unique. These can add a fun and quirky twist to your learning journey.

8. Plan Your Travels

One of the best ways to turn your retirement into an endless adventure is to plan out all the amazing places you want to visit. Grab some travel books, binge-watch travel videos, and chat with friends and family about their favorite destinations. Get inspired by their stories and suggestions!

> **Once you've got a list of must-see spots, it's time to get organized.**

Create a travel schedule and budget to make sure you can visit all these fantastic places without breaking the bank. Consider the best times to travel, look for deals on flights and accommodations, and maybe even join travel groups for retirees.

With a bit of planning, your dream adventures are *just around the corner*!

If you're looking for more specific ideas, we've got you covered. In Chapter 9, you'll find practical tips for planning your dream trips, discovering new destinations, and making the most of your travels. Whether you're jetting off to exotic lands or exploring hidden gems close to home, this chapter will guide you through organizing your travels, sticking to a budget, and ensuring every journey is as exciting and stress-free as possible.

9. Make Your Health Priority #1

Now that you're retired, it's time to give your health the VIP treatment it deserves. Start by scheduling those appointments you might have postponed while juggling work. Visit the doctor for a complete check-up, see the dentist for a sparkling smile, and don't forget the optometrist to keep your vision sharp.

Healthy eating is a game-changer, too. Incorporate more fruits, vegetables, whole grains, and lean proteins into your diet. Think colorful salads, hearty soups, and grilled fish. Enjoy those indulgent treats on special occasions but in moderation.

Exercise is another key ingredient for a vibrant retirement. Low-impact activities like walking, swimming, and yoga are perfect for staying active without straining your joints. Local community centers often offer classes, or you can explore online options if you prefer to work out at home.

Remember, this is *your time to enjoy life* to the fullest, and *staying healthy* is the best way to make that happen.

So, take care of yourself, embrace these healthy habits, and get ready to savor every moment of your well-deserved retirement!

THE BEST IS YET TO COME

You've reached the incredible milestone of retirement, a time to embrace life with enthusiasm and joy. It's like finally getting the backstage pass to a grand adventure where every day is filled with endless possibilities. This is your time to shine, explore, and live life to the fullest. After all the years of hard work, you deserve it!

As you embark on this new chapter, remember that a positive outlook can make all the difference. Don't think of retirement as an end but as a fantastic beginning. With a cheerful mindset, even the simplest activities can become extraordinary experiences. Whether you're discovering new hobbies, taking classes, or just enjoying a leisurely morning coffee, your positive attitude will transform these moments into cherished memories.

Now, let's talk about taking action. All those tips and activities we've discussed? They're your toolkit for an exciting and fulfilling retirement. Don't just read about them - jump in and try them! Create that bucket list, throw that fabulous retirement party, and explore those new hobbies. Each step will bring you closer to a life filled with excitement and satisfaction.

Remember, this is your time to indulge in *what makes you happy.*

There's no rush, no deadlines - just the wonderful opportunity to enjoy each day as it comes. Surround yourself with loved ones, laugh often, and keep an open mind to new adventures. The joy of retirement is in the journey, not just the destination.

So, go ahead and embrace your golden years with a heart full of enthusiasm and a spirit ready for fun. You've worked hard to get here; now it's time to savor every moment. Cheers to you and the fantastic adventures that await!

CHAPTER TWO

FINDING MY PURPOSE

Who Am I Without My Job?

Retirement is like the ultimate vacation - no more Monday blues, no deadlines, and you can finally say goodbye to those dreadful conference calls. But wait, what's this strange feeling creeping in? You might ask, "Who am I without my job?" Don't worry, you're not alone. Many retirees experience an identity crisis when they leave the workforce, and we're here to help you deal with this together.

Transitioning from working life to retirement can often lead to a sense of lost identity. Think about it: For decades, your job has been a huge part of your identity. You were Carlos, the Accountant; Priya, the Teacher; or Hans, the Engineer. Your professional identity was not just a title but a source of pride and purpose. Suddenly, that part of you is no longer there, and it's normal to feel a bit adrift.

Let's talk about some common pain points retirees face.

First, there's the loss of professional identity. Without your job, it might feel like a piece of you is missing. You might miss the routine, the structure, and even the office coffee machine that never worked quite right.

The lack of structure and routine is a big one. Remember when you used to dream about sleeping in? Now, with no alarm clock buzzing at 6 AM, you might feel like a ship without a compass. Routine gives our days shape and purpose; without it, time can start to feel like a never-ending Sunday. You find yourself struggling to remember what day it is.

Then there's the feeling of being without a true purpose. It's tough to go from being the go-to person at work to wondering if anyone still needs you. My retired nurse friend Yuki once said, "I used to save lives; now I save grocery coupons!" It's a funny way to look at it, but it highlights a genuine concern.

Less social interaction is another biggie. Work often provides a built-in social network. Without it, you might miss the camaraderie of colleagues and the daily connections that kept you engaged. My neighbor, Joseph, a retired chef, missed his kitchen crew so much that he started hosting weekly cook-offs just to stay social.

Finally, there are questions about what the future may hold. Without a clear roadmap, the endless possibilities of retirement can be both exciting and overwhelming. You've got all this time, but what should you do with it?

This is where the importance of self-reflection comes in.

Retirement is the perfect opportunity to step back and rediscover your inner values and passions. What makes you tick? What brings you joy? Think about what you loved doing as a child or the hobbies you've always wanted to try but never had the time for.

Remember, this is your time to shine. Embrace it with curiosity and an open heart. As you embark on this new journey, you'll find that retirement isn't about losing your identity but discovering new facets of yourself and finding renewed purpose. So, let's keep going, move forward, and explore together how to turn this identity crisis into the most exciting adventure of your life!

Who Am I Now?
Finding Your Purpose and Identity

Finding a new purpose and identity beyond your career is like discovering a hidden treasure chest—exciting and full of potential. Let's dig into how you can unearth this new sense of self.

First, discuss the theoretical framework behind finding purpose and identity. Psychologists tell us that a sense of purpose is crucial for our well-being. It gives us direction, motivation, and a reason to get out of bed in the morning (besides the smell of freshly brewed coffee, of course). When we retire, we must shift our focus from professional achievements to personal fulfillment.

One way to start this journey is through self-reflection. This might sound a bit like staring into the mirror and having a deep conversation with yourself - and in a way, it is. Grab a journal and ask yourself some big questions: What activities make you lose track of time? What were your childhood dreams? What values are most important to you? Writing down your thoughts can help clarify what truly matters to you.

Here's Isabella's story. She spent 30 years as a high-powered attorney, always in the fast lane. When she retired, she felt lost without her courtroom battles and legal briefs. Isabella started journaling and realized she missed her creative side. She had always loved painting but never had the time. She picked up a brush, joined a local art class, and found a new purpose in creating beautiful landscapes. Her paintings now grace the walls of local galleries, and she's never been happier.

Next, evaluate your personal strengths and interests. Think about what you're good at and what you enjoy doing. Maybe you were a project manager and loved organizing events. Why not channel that skill into planning community activities or volunteering for local charities? Or perhaps you were a teacher and have a passion for sharing knowledge. Consider tutoring or giving workshops on topics you love. You'll not only find sharing with others is rewarding, but you'll also find that you feel better about yourself with a new sense of accomplishment.

Self-acceptance is also key in this process. Embrace who you are now without the work title. It's a bit like trying on a new outfit - at first, it might feel strange, but soon you'll see it fits perfectly. Retirement is your chance to redefine your role in life. You're no longer bound by job descriptions, so let your imagination run wild and create a new place in the world for yourself!

Take, for example, Juan, who spent his career in finance. He always had a knack for storytelling, so he started writing children's books after retiring. His tales of adventurous animals brought him joy and delighted kids and parents alike. Juan discovered that his new role as an author was just as fulfilling as his previous career.

Another method is to explore new interests and hobbies. Attend workshops, try out different activities, and see what sparks joy within you. Don't be afraid to step out of your comfort zone - this is the perfect time to experiment and discover what you love.

Remember, finding a new purpose and identity *is a journey, not a sprint.*

It's about exploring different paths, trying new things, and rediscovering what makes you happy. So, embrace this opportunity with a joyful heart and an open mind. Your new identity is waiting to be discovered, and it will be amazing!

ACTIVITIES FOR UNCOVERING YOUR PURPOSE

Are you ready to try some fun and fulfilling activities to help you rediscover your sense of purpose? Whether you're looking to try new hobbies, set exciting goals, or learn something completely new and different, we've got all the ideas you need to get started. Let's find out what makes your heart sing in this exciting new chapter of your life!

1. Find a Purpose

Retirement is your golden opportunity to discover new purposes in life; trust me, it will be an adventure! Let's kick off this journey with some fun exercises and reflections to help you uncover what truly matters to you. Ready? Grab a comfy chair and a cup of your favorite drink, and let's get started!

01

THE JOY LIST

———

Start by making a list of activities that bring you joy. These don't have to be grand or elaborate; simple pleasures count too! Think about moments when you felt truly happy and fulfilled. Was it when you were gardening, baking, playing with your grandkids, or maybe volunteering at a local shelter? Write them all down. This joy list is your treasure map, guiding you toward what lights up your life.

02

REFLECT ON YOUR VALUES

———

Next, take some time to reflect on your core values. What principles have guided you throughout your life? Is it kindness, creativity, adventure, or perhaps learning? These values are the foundation of your new purpose. Grab that journal again and jot down your top five values. Seeing them in black and white can be incredibly enlightening.

THE "PERFECT DAY" VISUALIZATION

Close your eyes and imagine your perfect day in retirement. Where are you? What are you doing? Who are you with? This visualization helps you identify activities and routines that align with your ideal lifestyle. Once you've got a clear picture, write it down in detail. This exercise not only clarifies your desires but also helps set the stage for making them a reality.

SKILLS AND STRENGTHS INVENTORY

Think about all the skills and strengths you've accumulated over the years. You've got a lifetime of experience, and it's time to put it to good use. Make a list of your top skills and strengths. Are you great at organizing events or mentoring others? Maybe you have a knack for fixing things? Knowing what you're good at can help you find new ways to contribute and feel valuable.

You can find a template **HERE**

Finding What Matters.

Now, let's piece it all together. Look at your joy list, values, perfect day, and skills inventory. What patterns do you see? Maybe your love for gardening and your value of kindness leads you to start a community garden. Or perhaps your organizational skills and value of learning inspire you to set up local workshops. The goal is to find intersections that ignite excitement and fulfillment.

Don't be afraid to dip your toes into different activities to see what resonates. Volunteer at different places, join various clubs or start small projects. It's like trying on different hats until you find the one that fits perfectly. Remember, this is a journey, and there's no rush. Enjoy the process of discovering what makes your heart sing.

— 2. Discover and Pursue New Hobbies —

Retirement is your golden ticket to dive into hobbies old and new, turning free time into fun time! Whether you're rekindling a past passion or exploring something completely fresh, finding a new hobby can be one of the most amazing parts of this new stage of your life.

Start by making a list of things you've always been curious about but never had the time to pursue. Have you ever looked at a gorgeous painting and thought, "I'd love to try that?" Well, grab some brushes and let your creativity flow! Painting is a fantastic way to express yourself, relax, and create something beautiful. Start with a simple watercolor set, or take a local art class to get some tips.

Remember, there's no right or wrong way to paint - *just have fun with it!*

If you have a green thumb (or even if you don't!), gardening can be incredibly rewarding. There's something magical about nurturing plants and watching them grow. Whether you have a sprawling garden or just a few pots on your balcony, you can create a little oasis. Try growing your own vegetables, planting colorful flowers, or even starting a small herb garden. In addition, gardening gets you outside and moving, which is excellent for your health!

Have you always had a story to tell? Writing can be a fantastic way to share your thoughts, experiences, and imagination with the world. Start a blog, write a memoir, or even try your hand at fiction. The best part is that you don't need fancy equipment - just a pen and paper or a computer. Joining a writing group can also be a great way to get feedback and stay motivated.

For something a bit more unique, how about beekeeping? It's a fascinating hobby that connects you with nature and helps the environment. As an added bonus, you get to enjoy fresh honey! Another out-of-the-box idea is learning some fun and exciting magic tricks! Imagine the delight of entertaining your grandkids or friends with a bit of sleight of hand. You could also jump head-first into the world of drone flying, exploring new perspectives with aerial photography and videos.

Pursuing hobbies isn't just about filling your time. It's about *enriching your life*.

Hobbies bring a sense of accomplishment and joy. They provide a creative outlet and can be incredibly therapeutic. Hobbies often lead to meeting new people and forming new friendships. Imagine bonding with fellow gardeners over a particularly stubborn weed or sharing laughs with other writers at a local coffee shop. It's always helpful to be around like-minded people to inspire your confidence.

Not sure where to start? Think about what excites you. Have you always been fascinated by photography? Give it a shot! Curious about cooking? Try new recipes and maybe even take a cooking class. The key is experimenting and seeing what makes you passionate about life. Don't be afraid to step out of your comfort zone—you might just discover a new talent you never knew you had.

3. Join or Form a Hobby Group

Retirement is the perfect time to explore your passions, and what better way to enjoy your hobbies than by sharing them with others? Joining or forming a hobby group is a great way to meet new people, have fun, and stay engaged.

First, let's talk about joining existing hobby groups. These groups are everywhere - you just need to know where to look! Check out your local community centers, libraries, and online platforms like Meet-up.com or Facebook groups. Whether you're interested in knitting, bird-watching, or salsa dancing, a group of enthusiasts with similar interests will likely be nearby. If you love reading, book clubs are a great place to start. Enjoy hiking? Join a local hiking group and explore new trails with fellow nature lovers.

Now, if you can't find a group that fits your interests, why not start your own? It's easier than you might think. Begin by reaching out to friends, neighbors, and acquaintances who might share your hobby. Use social media to spread the word and create a simple flyer to post at local cafes, gyms, and community boards. Set a regular meeting time and place, and voila—you have a hobby group!

> **Here are some fun and hobby ideas you might want to consider:**

Urban Sketching

Grab a sketchbook and some pencils, and meet up with others to draw scenes from your city. It's a creative way to appreciate your surroundings and improve your art skills. This exploration could show you parts of your city that you never knew existed.

Brew Club

If you've ever been curious about brewing your own beer or making wine, this could be the hobby for you. Share recipes, taste each other's creations, and enjoy the process together.

Astronomy Club

Star-gazing is more fun with friends! Learn about constellations, planets, and galaxies while sharing telescopes and knowledge.

Cooking Exchange

Love to cook? Start a cooking group where members host and teach each other how to make their favorite dishes. You'll learn new recipes, and you'll get to enjoy delicious meals together!

Photography Walks

Grab your camera and join others on photo walks around different parts of town. Share tips, capture wondrous moments, and improve your photography skills. Again, you might learn something new about your city or area.

Practicing and enjoying hobbies with others has countless benefits. It keeps you socially active, which is great for mental health. It also provides a sense of community and belonging. Sharing your interests with others can lead to lasting friendships and fun memories. Plus, learning new skills and hobbies together can be incredibly motivating and inspiring.

4. Set New Challenges

Retirement is the perfect time to set new personal goals and challenges. Doing so keeps you engaged, motivated, and feeling alive! Setting challenges gives you a sense of purpose and achievement, making each day an exciting adventure.

Take this great guy, Larry, for example. Larry spent his career behind a desk and found that his fitness took a backseat to work like many of us. When he retired, he decided to take on a challenge to get in shape. With his doctor's approval, Larry started a fitness routine and, to everyone's amazement, set his sights on bodybuilding. Fast forward a year, and Larry got in shape and competed in a regional bodybuilding competition! His transformation was incredible, and his dedication inspired everyone around him.

Now, your challenges don't need to be as big as Larry's.

The key is to *start small* and *make fun, exciting challenges* that keep you moving ahead.

Maybe you've always wanted to learn to play the piano or run a 5K. Start with small, achievable goals like practicing for 15 minutes a day or walking a mile, and gradually increase your targets. These little victories build up and boost your confidence, pushing you to tackle bigger challenges.

Think about what excites you and set goals around those interests. Love reading? Challenge yourself to read a book a month. Enjoy cooking? Try making a new recipe every week. These challenges keep you engaged and add variety and spice to your daily routine.

Creating friendly competitions with yourself or friends can make goal-setting even more fun. Who can learn the most new dance moves in a month? Who can grow the biggest tomatoes in the garden? These light-hearted competitions add a layer of enjoyment and camaraderie.

Remember,
the purpose of
setting challenges
is to keep you
engaged and motivated.

It's about pushing your boundaries and discovering what you're capable of. So, think about what goals you'd like to achieve and start setting those challenges. Whether big or small, every challenge conquered is a step towards a more fulfilling and exciting retirement.

5. Do Something New Every Day

Retirement is your time of discovery, so why not add a dash of adventure by trying something new every day? It doesn't have to be anything grand - small, delightful changes can make a world of difference.

Imagine waking up each morning excited about a new experience waiting for you. It could be as simple as taking a different route on your morning walk, trying a new recipe for dinner, or learning a fun fact about a subject you're curious about. These little changes keep life interesting and help keep your mind engaged.

> ## Trying something new daily encourages you to step out of your comfort zone and *embrace the unknown*.

Remember the first time you tried sushi or attempted to dance the cha-cha? It might have felt awkward initially, but it was also thrilling, right? That's the magic of new experiences - they keep you on your toes and bring to your routine.

Here's a fun idea: Create a "New Experience Jar." Write down various activities, places to visit, or things to try on small pieces of paper and toss them into a jar. Each day, pick one out and let it guide your adventure. It could be anything from visiting a new café, planting a flower you've never grown, or even attempting a new craft.

Doing something new every day isn't just about keeping busy. It's about fostering a sense of adventure and continuous growth. It helps you discover new passions, meet interesting people, and see the world from different perspectives. Soon, you'll find it's a fantastic way to collect stories and experiences to share with friends and family.

For instance, my neighbor Anne decided to try a new hobby every week. One week, she was knitting scarves; the next, she was taking

French cooking classes. Her enthusiasm was infectious, and soon enough, a group of friends joined her in her weekly adventures. They even formed a club called "The Curious Crafters" and had the time of their lives exploring new activities together.

Remember, the goal is to *have fun* and keep the *spirit of curiosity* alive.

Whether learning a new word in a foreign language, trying a different type of exercise, or exploring a part of your town you've never been to, each new experience enriches your life and keeps you growing.

So, embrace the adventure and make it a habit to do something new daily. Your retirement is the perfect canvas for a life loaded with vibrant colors and exciting stories. Enjoy every moment of this journey, and let each day bring a delightful surprise!

6. Set Personal Goals

Retirement is your golden opportunity to set personal goals that bring a sense of purpose and joy to your days. Whether you want to learn a new skill, get fit, or travel more, setting goals gives you something exciting to work towards.

First,
let's talk about
the magic
of *SMART* goals.

SMART stands for Specific, Measurable, Achievable, Relevant, and Time-bound. This method helps you create clear and actionable goals. For example, instead of saying, "I want to get fit," try setting a SMART goal like, "I will walk for 30 minutes every morning for the next three months." This goal is specific, measurable, achievable, relevant, and time-bound.

Start with small goals to build momentum. Maybe you want to read more books. Begin with a goal to read one book a month. Once you're in the groove, you can aim higher, perhaps reading two or three books a month. These small victories boost your confidence and set the stage for tackling bigger goals.

Here are some tips to help you get started with goal setting:

Write It Down

Putting your goals on paper makes them feel real. It's incredibly satisfying to check them off as you achieve them. Create a goal journal where you can track your progress and reflect on your journey.

Break It Down

Large goals can be overwhelming, so break them into smaller, manageable steps. For instance, if your goal is to declutter your home, start with one room or even one drawer at a time.

Set Deadlines

Give yourself a timeline to work towards. This creates a sense of urgency and keeps you on track. Remember, deadlines can be flexible - adjust them as needed, but having a target date will help you maintain focus.

Celebrate Milestones

Don't wait until you've achieved the entire goal to celebrate. Acknowledge and reward yourself for the small milestones along the way. This keeps you motivated and makes the journey enjoyable.

Stay Flexible

Life is unpredictable, and adjusting your goals as you go is okay. Be open to changing your plans if necessary. The key is to keep moving forward, even if the path looks different than you initially envisioned.

I met an intelligent man named Miguel who always wanted to learn to play the guitar. His SMART goal was to practice for 20 minutes a day, five days a week, for six months. He started with simple chords and gradually moved on to playing complete songs. He set a small, achievable target each week, like learning a new chord or song section. By celebrating each milestone, Miguel stayed motivated, and now he's the star at our neighborhood jam sessions!

Remember, setting personal goals isn't just about achieving outcomes; it's about the *growth and joy* you experience along the way.

Each goal you set and accomplish adds a layer of fulfillment to your retirement years. So, dream big, start small, and let your goals guide you to a life filled with purpose and excitement.

7. Continue Learning and Share Knowledge

Retirement is the perfect time to become a lifelong learner. With endless opportunities to explore new subjects and share your wisdom, you can keep your mind sharp and engaged.

One of the most tremendous benefits of continuous learning is that it keeps your brain active and healthy. Just like your body needs exercise, your mind thrives on mental stimulation. Learning new things challenges your brain, improves memory, and can even delay the onset of cognitive decline. Overall, it's a fantastic way to satisfy your curiosity and discover new passions.

Imagine waking up each day with the excitement of *learning something new*.

It could be anything from mastering a new language to exploring the depths of astronomy. The beauty of retirement is that you have the time to dive into subjects that fascinate you. Sign up for online courses, attend local workshops, or simply pick up a book on a topic you've always wanted to explore.

A past co-worker, Helen, decided to learn Spanish after she retired. She started with a few apps like Duolingo and Babbel, and soon, she was chatting away with new friends worldwide. Daily practice sharpened her language skills and opened up a new cultural experience.

But learning isn't just about absorbing information - it's also about sharing what you know. Teaching others is a rewarding way to reinforce your own knowledge and keep your mind engaged. Consider starting a small study group, offering to tutor local students, or giving talks at community centers. Your life experiences and insights are invaluable; sharing them can make a big difference in someone else's life.

Take my neighbor, Tom. He's a retired engineer with a passion for woodworking. He started offering free woodworking classes in his garage. Now, he has a group of enthusiastic learners who gather weekly to create exciting and interesting projects. Not only does Tom enjoy teaching, but he's also made new friends and built a thriving community around his hobby.

Another fun way to share knowledge is through storytelling. Whether it's writing a blog, creating YouTube videos, or simply sharing stories with friends and family, your experiences can inspire and entertain others. Storytelling is a fantastic way to keep your mind active and engaged.

Learning and sharing are mutually beneficial. As you teach, you continually reinforce your understanding and discover new perspectives. It's a delightful cycle that keeps your brain buzzing with activity and your heart full of joy.

8. Adopt a Growth Mindset

Retirement is the perfect time to adopt a growth mindset, embracing challenges and viewing them as opportunities for growth. This positive outlook can transform your experiences, making each day a joyful adventure.

A growth mindset is all about believing that your abilities and intelligence can be developed through dedication and hard work. It's the opposite of a fixed mindset, which assumes our capabilities are set in stone.

> With a growth mindset,
> you see *challenges as chances*
> *to learn and improve*
> rather than obstacles to avoid.

Developing a growth mindset starts with changing the way you talk to yourself. Instead of saying, "I can't do this," try saying, "I can't do this yet." That little word, "yet," holds immense power. It opens the door to possibilities and encourages you to keep trying.

Nina used to be a neighbor of mine. When she retired, she decided to take up gardening despite having no prior experience. At first, her plants didn't thrive, and she felt frustrated. But instead of giving up, Nina embraced the challenge. She read gardening books, watched tutorials, and even joined a local gardening club. Over time, her garden flourished, and so did her confidence. Nina's growth mindset turned her initial failures into stepping stones for success.

Embracing challenges can be fun and rewarding. Start by setting small, achievable goals that push you out of your comfort zone. Maybe it's learning to play a musical instrument, tackling a new sport, or mastering a tech gadget. Each challenge you conquer builds resilience and boosts your self-esteem.

Remember, *mistakes* are part of the *learning process*.

Instead of viewing them as setbacks, see them as valuable feedback. When Thomas Edison was working on the lightbulb, he famously said, "I have not failed. I've just found 10,000 ways that won't work." Adopting this mindset can make your retirement years full of exciting discoveries and personal growth.

Engage in activities that stimulate your mind and encourage continuous learning. Take up puzzles, learn a new language, or dive into a complex craft project. These activities not only keep your brain active but also reinforce the belief that you can improve with effort.

Surround yourself with positive influences. Spend time with people who encourage your growth and share your enthusiasm for learning. Join clubs or groups that focus on self-improvement and shared interests. Positive reinforcement from like-minded individuals can strengthen your growth mindset.

Finally, celebrate your progress, no matter how small. Each step forward is a victory worth acknowledging. Keep a journal of your achievements and reflect on how far you've come. This practice reinforces the positive changes and keeps you motivated to continue growing.

Adopting a growth mindset transforms retirement into a period of dynamic learning and personal development. Embrace challenges joyfully, view setbacks as opportunities, and keep pushing your boundaries.

9. Learn New Things
Languages and Instruments

Retirement is the perfect time to expand your horizons by learning new things, and what better way to do that than by diving into languages and musical instruments? These pursuits are incredibly beneficial for your body and mind. Keeping your brain active is vital for maintaining mental sharpness and overall well-being. Learning new things stimulates your mind, boosts memory, and enhances cognitive function. It also brings a sense of accomplishment and joy, making your days more fulfilling and exciting.

Imagine being able to chat with locals on your next vacation, read foreign novels in their original language, or simply impress your friends with your multilingual skills.

Learning a new language opens up a *world of possibilities.*

It improves brain function, enhances problem-solving skills, and even delays the onset of dementia. It's a fantastic way to connect with different cultures and make new friends. Thanks to technology, learning a new language has never been easier. Apps like Babbel and Duolingo make the process fun and interactive. Daily lessons tailored to your skill level allow you to learn quickly and at your own pace. YouTube also offers many different language tutorials, and online courses can provide more structured learning. Pick a language that excites you, and start practicing today!

Playing a musical instrument is like a full-body workout for your brain. It enhances memory, sharpens concentration, and boosts creativity. Emotionally, it's a fantastic stress reliever and a way to express yourself. Whether you're strumming a guitar, tickling the ivories, or tapping out a rhythm on drums, making music brings great joy and satisfaction. There are countless resources available to help you learn an instrument. YouTube is a treasure trove of free tutorials for every instrument imaginable. Apps like Yousician provide interactive lessons and real-time feedback. You can also find online courses or hire a local tutor for personalized instruction. Start with an instrument that interests you, and enjoy the music-making journey.

A lady named Claudia always wanted to learn French but never had the time. With retirement, she downloaded Duolingo and started practicing every day. Now, she's not only fluent but also planning a trip to Paris to immerse herself in the culture. And then there's Jack, who picked up the saxophone at 65. He started with YouTube tutorials and eventually joined a local jazz group. Jack's new hobby has brought him endless joy and a whole new circle of friends.

Learning new languages and instruments adds layers of richness to your life. It keeps your mind sharp, opens new experiences, and brings joy and achievement. So, why not start today? Pick a language you've always wanted to learn or an instrument you've dreamed of playing. Dive in, have fun, and let your retirement be a symphony of new discoveries and extraordinary adventures. Enjoy every note and every word!

10. Share Your Journey

What better way to celebrate and share your experiences than by connecting with others? Whether through weekly meetups, giving talks, or creating a personal blog or vlog, sharing your journey can bring joy and inspiration to you and those around you.

Starting a blog or vlog is a fantastic way to document your adventures and interests. Imagine writing about your latest travel escapade, sharing gardening tips, or posting videos of your newly mastered yoga poses. Not only does this give you a creative outlet, but it also allows you to connect with a community of like-minded people who share your passions.

Let's look at Margie and her retirement journey. She started a travel blog detailing her RV trips across the country when she retired. Her humorous tales of road mishaps and hidden gems quickly gained a following. Now, Margie enjoys her travels more and loves interacting with her readers, who eagerly await her next post.

The benefits of documenting your journey are plentiful. It keeps your mind active, hones your writing or video editing skills, and provides a sense of accomplishment. It's a purposeful way to reflect on your experiences and see how far you've come.

> ## Each post or video becomes a *cherished memory* you can *reflect on with pride.*

If blogging or vlogging isn't your style, consider having weekly meetups with friends or community members. These gatherings include casual coffee chats, book club meetings, or hobby groups. Sharing your stories and hearing about others' adventures creates a supportive network that keeps you engaged and socially active.

Giving talks at local community centers or libraries is another excellent way to share your journey. Whether you're an expert knitter, a history buff, or a seasoned traveler, your knowledge and experiences can inspire and educate others. This is also an excellent way to build confidence and public speaking skills.

Let's not forget about the power of technology.

Platforms like Facebook, Instagram, and YouTube make sharing your journey with a global audience easy. You can post photos, write updates, and connect with people from all over the world who share your interests. The connections you make can lead to lasting friendships and even collaborations on projects you're passionate about.

So, grab your laptop, camera, or simply a cup of coffee with a friend, and start sharing your journey. Your stories, experiences, and insights are valuable. They can brighten someone's day and also leave a lasting legacy for future generations to look back on. The joy and fulfillment you'll gain from connecting with others will make your retirement even more rewarding.

EMBRACING YOUR NEW IDENTITY AND PURPOSE

Congratulations! You've reached the end of this chapter and taken the first steps toward embracing your new identity and purpose in retirement. Let's take a moment to recap the key points we've covered and inspire you to jump feet-first into this exciting phase of your life with enthusiasm and joy.

First, we explored the concept of an identity crisis in retirement and how feeling a bit lost without your professional title is entirely normal. But as we've discovered, retirement is not the end of your story—it's the beginning of a thrilling new chapter. Through self-reflection and understanding your core values, you can uncover what truly matters to you and set the foundation for a new and fulfilling life.

We talked about finding new purpose by exploring and pursuing hobbies that bring you joy, joining or forming hobby groups to share your interests with others, and setting personal challenges to keep yourself motivated. Remember Larry, who transformed his fitness journey into a regional bodybuilding competition? His story shows that with a growth mindset, the sky's the limit!

You've also learned about the joy of trying something new every day, fostering a sense of adventure, and keeping life exciting. From mastering a new language with Duolingo to strumming a guitar with YouTube tutorials, continuous learning keeps your mind sharp and your heart happy.

We highlighted the importance of sharing your journey through weekly meetups, giving talks, or starting a blog or vlog. Whether you're Margie, who entertains her readers with RV tales, or Tom, who inspires a community with woodworking classes, sharing your experiences enriches both your life and the lives of others.

Now, as you stand on the threshold of this incredible new phase, remember to embrace it with open arms and a joyful heart.

This is your time to *rediscover who you are* beyond your career.

It's your chance to pursue passions, learn new skills, and connect with amazing people.

Life after retirement
is not just about filling your days;
it's about *finding fulfillment*
in every moment.

Embrace challenges as opportunities for growth, celebrate your achievements, no matter how small, and always keep an open mind. You are capable of wonderful things; this is your time to shine.

So go ahead and write your own story filled with laughter, love, and endless adventures. Rediscover your sense of self and purpose, and let each day be a testament to your amazing journey. Your retirement years are a precious gift—unwrap them enthusiastically and enjoy every delightful moment.

Cheers to you
and the incredible adventures ahead!

Suggested Reading List

Diving into a good book is a fantastic way to expand your horizons and discover new passions. Here's a reading list to help you develop a growth mindset, find joy, and build positive habits in your retirement.

Each book offers *valuable insights and inspiration* to make the most of this exciting new chapter.

"Mindset: The New Psychology of Success"
by Carol S. Dweck

 This book is a gem! Carol Dweck explores the power of a growth mindset - believing that abilities and intelligence can be developed through dedication and hard work. With engaging anecdotes and research-backed insights, she shows how adopting a growth mindset can lead to success and fulfillment in all areas of life. Get ready to see challenges as opportunities and embrace lifelong learning.

"The Happiness Project"
by Gretchen Rubin

 Join Gretchen Rubin on her year-long journey to discover what truly makes her happy. Rubin experiments with various happiness strategies in this charming and relatable book, from decluttering her home to cultivating gratitude. Her practical tips and humorous observations will inspire you to embark on your own happiness project and find more joy in everyday moments.

"The Power of Now: A Guide to Spiritual Enlightenment"
by Eckhart Tolle

 Eckhart Tolle's classic guide to living in the present moment is a must-read. He teaches us how to let go of past regrets and future anxieties to fully embrace the now. With profound yet accessible wisdom, Tolle encourages us to find peace and purpose by being present. It's a beautiful reminder to savor each day of your retirement.

"Atomic Habits: An Easy & Proven Way to Build Good Habits & Break Bad Ones"
by James Clear

 James Clear offers a practical and engaging approach to building habits that stick. Learn how small changes can lead to remarkable results. Clear's strategies are easy to implement and backed by scientific research. Whether you want to start a new hobby, improve your health, or simply get more organized, this book provides the tools to make lasting positive changes.

"Big Magic: Creative Living Beyond Fear"
by Elizabeth Gilbert

 Elizabeth Gilbert, author of "Eat, Pray, Love," dives into the world of creativity and inspiration. "Big Magic" encourages you to embrace curiosity, tackle what you love, and let go of perfectionism. Gilbert's joyful and motivating advice will help you unleash your creative potential and live a more vibrant, fearless life.

„Ikigai: The Japanese Secret to a Long and Happy Life"
by Héctor García and Francesc Miralles

Explore the Japanese concept of ikigai, which means "a reason for being." This beautiful book looks into finding purpose and happiness through activities that give your life meaning. Filled with insights from the residents of Okinawa, the world's longest-living people, "Ikigai" offers practical tips on discovering and pursuing your own ikigai.

"The Art of Possibility: Transforming Professional and Personal Life"
by Rosamund Stone Zander and Benjamin Zander

This uplifting book combines art, science, and personal growth. The Zanders present twelve practices to help you shift your perspective, embrace creativity, and seize opportunities. Their inspiring stories and actionable advice make "The Art of Possibility" a fantastic guide to transforming your life.

CHAPTER THREE

BOREDOM
BUSTERS

Fun at Home

Retirement can sometimes bring unexpected challenges, like feeling a bit empty or lacking the social interaction you once had at work. Maybe you've felt your motivation wane or slipped into passivity, wondering how to fill those extra hours. But fear not! This is your time to rediscover passions you might have put on the back burner, all from the comfort of your own home.

Let's address some issues head-on. Feeling empty? Let's fill that space with joy and purpose through creative home projects. Lack of social interaction? There are endless ways to connect with others, even from your living room, through virtual meetups, online classes, and social media groups. Struggling with motivation? We have plenty of tips to inspire you with home-based activities that spark joy. And as for passivity, we will turn that into proactivity with a whole bunch of engaging home activities.

> One of the greatest gifts of retirement is the *freedom to explore*, especially within your own space.

Remember that skill you always wanted to learn but couldn't fit into your busy schedule? Now's the time to dive in, right in your kitchen, living room, or backyard! Retirement offers a golden opportunity to discover new interests and revive old passions. Whether it's starting DIY projects in your garage, launching a small home-based business from your study, or simply staying mentally sharp with puzzles and games in the family room, the possibilities within your home are endless and exciting.

I spoke to a lady named Joan at a local meetup group. After retiring, she felt a bit lost without her daily work routine. But then she dusted off her old paintbrushes and rediscovered her love for painting.

Now, she spends her afternoons creating art in her home studio. She even joined an online art community where she shares her work and makes new friends. Joan's days are now filled with color, creativity, and connection, all from the comfort of her home.

So, let's begin our trek on this delightful journey together. This chapter contains ideas and inspiration to keep you entertained and fulfilled at home. From gaming and gardening to woodworking and blogging, there's something here for everyone. Get ready to turn your home into a hub of fun and excitement, making every day of your retirement an adventure!

Avoiding Boredom and Staying Entertained at Home:

Being retired is similar to having a never-ending weekend, but those days can start feeling too long without a plan. Staying active and engaged at home is key to ensuring your retirement is as vibrant and joyful as you've imagined. So, let's see why keeping busy is so important and how you can make every day new and exciting.

First and foremost, staying active and engaged is crucial for your mental and emotional well-being. When you're busy with creative projects or new challenges, there's no room for boredom to sneak in. Your brain loves a good workout, and learning something new or tackling a fun project keeps it sharp and happy. Think of your mind as a garden; it needs regular watering and care to stay lush and green. By staying engaged, you're giving your brain the nutrients it needs to thrive.

Creative projects are a fantastic way to keep boredom at bay. Whether knitting a cozy blanket, painting a masterpiece, or building a birdhouse, these activities provide a sense of accomplishment and purpose. Let's be honest; they're just plain fun! When you're immersed in a creative project, time flies, leaving you with something beautiful or useful to show for your efforts.

New challenges are another great way to stay entertained. Set yourself small, achievable goals and relish the thrill of conquering them.

Maybe you've always wanted to learn to play the piano or cook a gourmet meal. Taking on these challenges keeps you engaged, boosts your confidence, and gives you stories to share with friends and family.

An active lifestyle isn't just good for your mind - it's great for your body, too. Regular physical activity, whether gardening, dancing, or a daily walk, keeps you fit and energized. It's also an excellent way to lift your spirits. Physical activity releases endorphins, the body's natural mood lifters, making you feel happier and more relaxed. You'll sleep better at night, so you wake up refreshed and ready to seize the day.

Boredom Tips and Strategies

Staying active and engaged at home requires a bit of planning and inspiration. Here are some practical tips and strategies to help you manage your time, stay motivated, and find the resources you need to make your retirement as fulfilling and joyful as possible.

Time Management: Structuring Your Day

Creating a daily schedule is one of the best ways to ensure you make the most of your time. Start by setting aside specific blocks of time for different activities. For instance, you might dedicate mornings to exercise or gardening, afternoons to creative projects like painting or woodworking, and evenings to relaxing activities such as reading or watching a favorite show.

01 Use a planner or digital calendar to block out time for various activities. Seeing your day mapped out visually can help you stick to your plans.

Include buffer times between activities to allow for breaks and flexibility. This prevents you from feeling rushed and helps you enjoy each activity more. 02

03 Prioritize activities that bring you joy and fulfillment. This ensures that you look forward to your day and stay motivated.

Finding Motivation: Staying Inspired

Keeping yourself motivated can sometimes be challenging, but with a few strategies, you can stay inspired and excited about your daily activities.

01 Set small, achievable goals. Breaking larger projects into smaller tasks makes them less daunting and more manageable. For example, if you want to write a memoir, start with one chapter at a time.

Reward yourself for completing tasks. Treat yourself to a favorite snack, a relaxing bath, or a new book once you've accomplished a goal.

03 Surround yourself with positivity. Create a motivational board with quotes, photos, and reminders of your goals. Place it somewhere you'll see it often to keep your spirits high.

Utilizing Resources: Finding Support and Ideas

There are so many resources available to help you stay active and engaged. Here are some recommendations to get you started:

Check out "The Life-Changing Magic of Tidying Up" by Marie Kondo for inspiration on decluttering and organizing, or "Creative Confidence" by Tom Kelley and David Kelley for boosting your creativity.

Visit Pinterest for DIY project ideas and tutorials, or join online communities like Reddit for DIY tips and support from fellow enthusiasts.

Look for local clubs or groups that align with your interests. Many communities offer gardening clubs, book clubs, and crafting groups. Libraries and community centers often host events and workshops that can provide new ideas and social opportunities.

EXCITING ACTIVITIES FOR YOUR RETIREMENT ADVENTURE

Let's dive head-first into a variety of activities designed to keep you entertained, mentally active, and full of joy. We'll explore everything from gardening to gaming, blogging, and launching a small business. Whether you're a fan of video games, have a green thumb, or are itching to start a new DIY project, we've got you covered.

1. Gaming
Fun and Games to Keep You Sharp

Who says games are just for kids? Retirement is the perfect time to rediscover the joy of gaming, and it's a fantastic way to stay entertained and mentally active. Whether you prefer the tactile feel of a classic board game or the high-tech excitement of video games, there's something here to tickle your fancy.

Engaging in games isn't just fun - it's also *great for your brain*.

Games challenge your mind, improve your memory, and sharpen your cognitive skills. They're a fantastic way to spend time with family and friends or make new connections online.

Let's start with some board games. Classics like Scrabble and Chess never go out of style and are perfect for keeping your mind agile. If you're looking for something a bit different, try Ticket to Ride, a delightful game where you build train routes across the country. For a more strategic challenge, Settlers of Catan will have you trading resources and building settlements in no time.

Prefer to go digital? There are plenty of video games and apps designed for all ages. Brain Age and Lumosity offer fun puzzles and activities specifically aimed at boosting brain function. For some adventure, try Animal Crossing, a charming game where you can create your own island paradise, make friends, and collect treasures. If you're a fan of puzzles, Candy Crush Saga is both addictive and highly satisfying.

Online games are another great option, offering endless opportunities for fun and interaction. Words with Friends is a popular choice that lets you challenge friends or strangers to a word-building game.

If you're feeling competitive, explore the world of online chess or bridge clubs. These games keep you entertained and connect you with a global community of gamers.

For those who enjoy computer games, The Sims allows you to build and manage your own virtual world. At the same time, Stardew Valley offers a relaxing farming simulation with plenty of activities to keep you busy. And don't forget about trivia games like Trivia Crack, which test your knowledge on a wide range of topics and can be played solo or with friends.

Whatever game you choose, the key is to *have fun and enjoy the challenge.*

Gaming is a fantastic way to keep your mind active, stay socially connected, and add a dose of excitement to your day. So, dust off those board games, charge up your tablet, and get ready to play!

2. Gardening

Cultivate Joy and Health in Your Own Backyard

Ready to turn your backyard into a paradise? Gardening is a fun way to spend your time and offers incredible benefits for your physical and mental health. So grab your gardening gloves, and let's dig into the joys of cultivating your own green oasis!

Starting a garden is a great way to enjoy the outdoors and connect with nature. Whether you're planting vibrant flowers, juicy vegetables, or aromatic herbs, gardening can transform your space into a colorful and serene retreat. Imagine stepping outside each morning to the sight of blooming roses or the taste of freshly picked tomatoes. It's pure bliss!

Gardening isn't just about creating beauty; it's also fantastic for your body. All that digging, planting, and weeding provides a great workout, helping to keep you fit and flexible. It's a low-impact activity that can improve your strength, endurance, and cardiovascular health. As an additional benefit, spending time in the sun helps your body produce vitamin D, which is essential for bone health.

On top of the physical benefits, gardening does wonders for your mental well-being. Nurturing plants and watching them grow can be incredibly satisfying and therapeutic. It gives you a sense of purpose and accomplishment, reducing stress and promoting relaxation. There's something magical about the rhythm of tending to your garden that can melt away worries and bring a sense of calm.

Take this amazing woman, Veronica, for instance. After retiring, she started a small vegetable garden and found it the perfect way to unwind. She loves the quiet time spent with her plants and the joy of harvesting her own produce. Subsequently, she's become the neighborhood expert on all things green, sharing tips and homegrown goodies with friends and family.

Gardening also keeps your mind sharp. Planning your garden layout, researching the best plants for your region, and learning about soil health and pest control all engage your brain in a meaningful way. It's a fantastic way to stay connected with others. Join a local gardening club, attend workshops, or participate in community garden projects to meet fellow enthusiasts and exchange ideas.

If you're new to gardening, start small. You don't need a large yard to enjoy the benefits; even a few pots on a balcony can be transformed into a mini-garden. Choose plants that are easy to grow and maintain, such as basil, marigolds, or cherry tomatoes. As you gain confidence and experience, you can expand your garden and experiment with different plants and techniques.

3. Be Creative
DIY Projects

Who's ready to unleash their inner artist and handyperson? Undertaking DIY projects is a fantastic way to stay busy, add a personal touch to your home, and have a lot of fun in the process. Let's discover how you can transform everyday items into masterpieces!

DIY projects are an amazing way to channel your creativity and produce something beautiful and functional. The possibilities are endless, whether you're refurbishing old furniture, crafting unique decorations, or building handy household items.

> There's nothing quite like the satisfaction of saying, *"I made that!"*

To get started, think about what interests you the most. Do you love painting, building, or crafting? Once you've identified your passion, there are countless projects to choose from.

Let's explore a few ideas to spark your creativity:

Furniture Makeovers

Have an old chair or table that's seen better days? Give it a fresh look with a coat of paint, new upholstery, or a fun stencil design. There are plenty of YouTube tutorials that walk you through the process step-by-step. Check out "DIY Creators" or "The Rehab Life" channels for inspiration and guidance.

Homemade Decorations

From seasonal wreaths to personalized photo frames, creating your own home decor is both fun and rewarding. Try making a rustic picture frame using reclaimed wood or crafting a beautiful wreath with faux flowers and a hot glue gun. Pinterest is a treasure trove of ideas and tutorials for every skill level.

Garden Projects

Combine your love of gardening with DIY by building a raised garden bed, creating decorative plant markers, or constructing a birdhouse. Websites like "The Spruce Crafts" and "HGTV" offer easy-to-follow guides and innovative ideas for garden-related projects.

Upcycled Crafts

Turn everyday items into treasures with upcycling. Transform glass jars into chic storage containers, or repurpose an old ladder into a stylish bookshelf. The possibilities are endless, and you'll be doing your part for the environment by reducing waste.

Wall Art

Bring color and personality to your home with DIY wall art. Paint a canvas with abstract designs, create a collage of your favorite photos, or try your hand at string art. Channels like "Crafty Panda" on YouTube offer fun and easy tutorials to get you started.

Home Improvements

If you feel ambitious, tackle some home improvement projects. Install new shelves, build a custom closet organizer, or create a cozy reading nook. Websites like "DIY Network" provide comprehensive guides for various home improvement tasks.

The beauty of DIY projects is that they're as varied as your imagination allows. They keep your hands busy, your mind engaged, and your creativity flowing. They're a fantastic way to personalize and make your living space uniquely yours.

So, roll up your sleeves, gather your materials, and *let your creativity run wild.*

Whether crafting, building, or painting, DIY projects are a fun way to spend time creating something extraordinary.

4. Drawing and Painting
Unleash Your Inner Artist

Ready to paint the town red - or perhaps a serene landscape? Drawing and painting are fantastic ways to explore your artistic side and bring a splash of color into your life. Let's keep going and jump right into the world of art, discover the joy of creating, and uncover some great resources to get you started!

There's something magical about putting pencil to paper or brush to canvas. It's a form of expression that allows you to capture your thoughts, feelings, and imagination in a way that words often can't. Whether sketching a bowl of fruit or painting a vibrant sunset, drawing, and painting can transport you to a world of creativity and wonder.

Not only are these activities incredibly fun, but they're also therapeutic. Creating art can reduce stress, improve focus, and promote mindfulness. When deeply engrossed in your work, worries seem to melt away, replaced by a calming sense of accomplishment.

Think of it
as yoga for the mind,
*stretching your creativity
and relaxing your thoughts.*

If you're new to drawing and painting, don't worry! You don't need to be the next Picasso to enjoy the benefits. Start with simple sketches. Grab a sketchbook and a set of pencils, and begin with basic shapes and lines. YouTube channels like "Draw with Jazza" offer easy tutorials for beginners. Websites like "Sketchbook Skool" provide structured courses that guide you through the basics and beyond.

When it comes to painting, you can choose between watercolors, acrylics, or oils. Watercolors are great for beginners due to their forgiving nature. Acrylics dry quickly and are perfect for vibrant, layered works. Oils are rich and blend beautifully but require a bit more patience. For beginners, "The Art Sherpa" on YouTube offers step-by-step tutorials in acrylics. At the same time, "Lena Danya" provides tips for watercolor painting.

Invest in a good set of brushes, quality paper or canvas, and a palette of colors. Online art supply stores like Blick or local craft shops often have starter kits. Many communities also offer beginner art classes - check out local community centers, art schools, or even online platforms like Skillshare and Udemy for structured lessons.

Like any skill, art improves with practice. Dedicate a little time each day to drawing or painting. Keep a daily sketch journal, participate in monthly art challenges, or join online art communities to share your work and get feedback.

Remember,
the journey is just as important
as the destination,
so *enjoy each stroke and sketch.*

5. Start a Blog or YouTube Channel
Share Your Story with the World

Have you ever thought about starting a blog or YouTube channel? It's a fantastic way to share your stories, experiences, and hobbies with the world. You'll discover it's a great way to connect with others who share your passions.

Starting a blog or YouTube channel allows you to express yourself and share your unique perspective. Whether you're documenting your travels, sharing delicious recipes, or showcasing your latest DIY project, there's an audience out there eager to hear from you. Your experiences and insights are valuable; you never know who you might inspire or connect with through your posts and videos.

Blogs are a great platform if you love to write. You can create a blog on platforms like WordPress, Blogger, or Medium. Choose a theme that reflects your personality, and start posting! You can write about anything that interests you - gardening tips, book reviews, travel diaries, or even funny anecdotes from your daily life. The key is to be authentic and have fun with it.

If you're more comfortable in front of a camera, starting a YouTube channel might be the way to go. It's a fantastic platform for visual storytelling. You can create how-to videos, vlogs, cooking tutorials, or even share your fitness journey. Platforms like YouTube offer a broad audience, and your content can reach people from all over the globe. The help of video editing software like iMovie or Adobe Premiere makes it easy to create professional-looking videos, even if you're a beginner.

One of the best things about blogging or vlogging is the community you build. By sharing your passions, you'll connect with others with similar interests. Readers and viewers can comment on your posts, share their experiences, and offer advice and encouragement. This interaction creates a sense of belonging and makes the whole experience even more rewarding.

6. Go on Adventures
Discover Fun Around Every Corner

Retirement is the perfect time to embark on new adventures, big and small! There's a whole world of excitement waiting just outside your door, and you don't have to go far to find it.

> **Let's explore the endless possibilities for adventures that will keep you entertained and engaged.**

Have you ever tried geocaching? It's like a modern-day treasure hunt that's fun for all ages. Using a GPS or smartphone, you can search for hidden "caches" that other adventurers have tucked away in parks, forests, and urban areas. Each cache contains a logbook to sign; some even have little trinkets you can trade. It's a fantastic way to explore your local surroundings and exercise while you're at it.

If you prefer something more relaxed, how about a walking tour of your town or city? Even if you've lived there for years, you'd be surprised at how many hidden gems you might discover. Visit local museums, historical landmarks, or quirky cafes you've never tried. You can even make a game of it—try to find the best cappuccino in town or the most exciting piece of street art.

For those who love nature, hiking is an exciting adventure combining physical activity and breathtaking scenery. Find a nearby trail and immerse yourself in the beauty of the great outdoors. Don't forget to bring a picnic lunch to enjoy at a scenic spot along the way. Bird-watching is another excellent way to connect with nature. Grab a pair of binoculars and a guidebook, and see how many different species you can spot.

If you're a fan of puzzles and challenges, escape rooms are a thrilling adventure you can enjoy with friends or family. These themed rooms require you to solve a series of puzzles to "escape" within a set time limit. It's a great way to exercise your brain and have fun.

Consider joining a local club or group that aligns with your interests for something truly unique. Love photography? Join a photography club and go on photo walks with fellow enthusiasts. Fascinated by history? Look for a local historical society that offers tours and lectures. These groups are a fantastic way to meet new people and discover new hobbies.

Exploring your local area can lead to *unexpected adventures.*

Visit a nearby farmers market and sample fresh, local produce. Attend a community theater performance or an outdoor concert. Check out local festivals and fairs—they often feature interesting crafts, delicious food, and lively entertainment.

7. Woodwork/Handcrafting
Crafting Joy with Your Own Hands

Ready to channel your inner craftsman or craftswoman? Taking up woodworking or other handcrafting activities is a fantastic way to stay busy, creative, and fulfilled. There's nothing quite like the satisfaction of creating something beautiful and functional with your own hands.

Woodworking is a *timeless hobby* that combines skill, creativity, and a bit of elbow grease.

Imagine turning a simple piece of wood into a charming birdhouse, a sturdy bookshelf, or even a handcrafted cutting board. The possibilities are endless, and each project you complete adds a unique, personal touch to your home.

Handcrafting isn't just about making items; it's about the joy and pride of creating something from scratch. There's a special kind of magic in seeing your vision come to life, piece by piece. Working with your hands is great for your mental well-being. It's a meditative process that helps you focus, reduces stress, and gives you a wonderful sense of accomplishment.

If you're new to woodworking, start with some simple projects that don't require a lot of tools or experience.

Here are a few ideas to spark your creativity:

Birdhouse

A classic beginner project, a birdhouse is fun to build and provides a cozy home for your feathered friends. Plenty of templates and tutorials online guide you through the process.

Picture Frames

Crafting your own picture frames is a great way to showcase your favorite photos. You can keep the design simple or add decorative touches like paint or carvings.

Planter Boxes

Build a wooden planter box to spruce up your garden or patio. This project is straightforward and allows for lots of creativity in terms of size, shape, and finish.

Shelving Units

Start small with a simple wall-mounted shelf, or go bigger with a multi-tiered bookshelf. Shelves are practical projects that can be customized to fit your space perfectly.

Coasters and Cutting Boards

These excellent beginner projects make terrific gifts. Additionally, they give you the opportunity to experiment with different types of wood and finishes.

To get started, look for online tutorials and classes on platforms like YouTube, Skillshare, or local community centers. Websites like "Woodworkers Guild of America" and "Instructables" offer detailed guides and project ideas for all skill levels. Joining a local woodworking or crafting group can also be a great way to learn new techniques, share tips, and make new friends.

8. Photography
Capture the World and Share Your Vision

Grab your camera and get ready to see the world through a new lens! Photography is a thrilling hobby that lets you capture the beauty around you and share your unique perspective. Photography is a fantastic way to stay engaged and creatively fulfilled, whether snapping shots of nature, family moments, or bustling cityscapes.

Photography is more than just taking pictures; it's about *telling a story*.

Each click of the shutter captures a moment in time, a piece of your world that you can share with others. It's a joyful way to express your creativity and explore your surroundings, finding beauty in the everyday.

To get started, you don't need a fancy camera - a smartphone with a good camera will do just fine. The key is to start experimenting and learning the basics. Focus on composition, lighting, and perspective. Try taking photos from different angles, playing with shadows and light, and framing your shots to highlight your subject.

One of the best ways to improve your photography skills is to practice regularly. Set yourself small challenges, like capturing a photo a day or focusing on a particular theme each week. This keeps you motivated and helps you see progress over time. Joining a photography group or taking an online course can also provide valuable tips and feedback. Websites like "Udemy," "Skillshare," and YouTube channels such as "Digital Photography School" offer excellent tutorials for photographers of all levels.

Here are some tips to take your photography to the next level:

01

EXPERIMENT WITH SETTINGS

If you're using a digital camera, learn about the different settings, like aperture, shutter speed, and ISO. Experimenting with these can drastically change the look and feel of your photos.

02

EDIT YOUR PHOTOS

Post-processing can enhance your images and highlight details you might have missed. Software like Adobe Lightroom or free apps like Snapseed offer powerful editing tools that are easy to use.

03

STUDY GREAT PHOTOGRAPHERS

Look at the work of professional photographers for inspiration. Notice how they compose their shots, use lighting, and capture emotions. You can find many examples in photography books, online galleries, and social media platforms like Instagram.

JOIN A PHOTOGRAPHY COMMUNITY

Sharing your work and getting feedback from others can be incredibly motivating. Join local photography clubs, participate in online forums, or follow photography hashtags on social media to connect with fellow enthusiasts.

ENTER CONTESTS

Many websites and organizations host photography contests. Entering these can push you to improve your skills and give you a sense of accomplishment. It's fun to see how your work stacks up against others.

> Sharing photos online
> is a wonderful way
> to *connect with others*
> and *showcase your talent.*

Create an Instagram account dedicated to your photography, start a blog, or join photo-sharing websites like Flickr or 500px. Each platform offers a unique way to share your work, get feedback, and find inspiration from other photographers.

9. Starting a Business
Turn Your Passion into Profit

Ready to turn your hobbies into a little extra income? Starting a small home-based business is a fantastic way to stay engaged, keep your mind active, and earn money. Whether you're into crafting, pet sitting, or baking, a business opportunity awaits you. Let's explore how you can launch your venture and enjoy the rewarding entrepreneurship journey.

First things first: think about what you love doing. The best businesses are built on passion, so choose something that excites you. Are you a whiz with knitting needles? Do you have a knack for baking the most delicious cookies? Maybe you're an animal lover who would enjoy pet sitting. Whatever your interest, there's a market out there for it.

> Once you've decided
> on your business idea,
> *it's time to get started.*

Here are some tips to help you launch your home-based business:

☐ **Research Your Market**

Understand who your potential customers are and what they're looking for. Check out similar businesses, both local and online, to see what's already out there and how you can stand out.

☐ **Create a Business Plan**

It doesn't have to be fancy, but having a plan helps you stay organized and focused. Outline your goals, target market, pricing strategy, and marketing plan. Websites like "SCORE" offer free templates and resources to help you draft your plan.

☐ Set Up Your Workspace

Designate a space in your home where you can work without distractions. Make sure it's comfortable and equipped with everything you need. Whether it's a craft table in the spare room or a corner in the kitchen, having a dedicated workspace helps you stay productive.

☐ Start Small

You don't need a huge investment to get started. Begin with what you have and gradually invest in more supplies or equipment as your business grows. For example, if you're starting a crafting business, begin with a few essential products and expand your offerings over time.

☐ Promote Your Business

Spread the word about your new venture! Create social media accounts to showcase your products or services, join local business groups, and consider setting up an online store on platforms like Etsy or eBay. Word of mouth is powerful, so tell friends and family about your business and ask them to help spread the word.

☐ Provide Excellent Service

Happy customers are the best advertisement. Ensure you're providing high-quality products or services and excellent customer service. Respond promptly to inquiries, be polite, and go the extra mile to make your customers feel valued.

☐ Learn and Adapt

Keep an eye on what works and what doesn't. Be open to feedback and willing to make changes as needed. Continuous learning is key to running a successful business. Consider taking online courses on websites like "Udemy" or "Coursera" to improve your skills.

My sister's best friend, Susan, turned her love for baking into a small home-based business. Starting with just a few recipes, she sold her delicious treats to friends and neighbors. Word spread, and soon, she got orders from all over town. Susan now has a thriving business, all run from her cozy kitchen.

Starting a business can be *incredibly fulfilling*.

It keeps you engaged, provides a creative outlet, and allows you to share your passion with others. And the extra income is always a nice bonus! So, think about what you love doing, take that first step, and enjoy the journey of entrepreneurship. You never know where it might lead.

10. Cooking and Baking
Whip Up Joy in Your Kitchen

Ready to add some spice to your life? Cooking and baking are fantastic ways to experiment, create, and have fun right in your kitchen. Whether you're a seasoned chef or a newbie in the kitchen, there's always something new to learn and enjoy.

Cooking and baking bring joy in countless ways. There's the satisfaction of creating something from scratch, the delight of tasting your creations, and the pleasure of sharing them with loved ones. Imagine the aroma of freshly baked bread wafting through your home or the excitement of trying a new dish that turns out perfectly. It's pure, tasty bliss!

Experimenting with new recipes is an excellent way to *keep things interesting* in the kitchen.

Start by exploring cuisines you've never tried before. Ever made Thai curry from scratch? How about an authentic Italian lasagna? Dive into cookbooks, food blogs, and YouTube channels for inspiration. Websites like AllRecipes and Epicurious offer endless recipe ideas for all skill levels.

Joining online cooking classes or groups is a fantastic way to improve your culinary skills and meet fellow food enthusiasts. Platforms like MasterClass, Udemy, and even YouTube offer classes taught by professional chefs. You can learn everything from basic knife skills to advanced pastry techniques. Many online cooking communities and forums allow you to share your progress, ask for advice, and get inspired by others' creations.

Here are some tips to get the most out of your cooking and baking adventures:

01

START SIMPLE

———

Don't feel like you must tackle a five-course meal immediately. Begin with simple recipes that interest you. As you build confidence, you can try more complex dishes.

02

HAVE FUN WITH IT

———

Cooking and baking should be enjoyable, not stressful. Put on some music, pour a glass of wine, and enjoy the process. Remember, you've still learned something new even if a dish doesn't turn out perfectly.

03

EXPERIMENT

———

Don't be afraid to tweak recipes to suit your taste. Add a little more spice, swap out ingredients, or try a new cooking method. This experimentation can lead to delightful culinary discoveries.

04

JOIN A COOKING GROUP

Many communities have cooking clubs or groups that meet regularly to cook and share meals together. If you prefer to stay online, join cooking forums or social media groups where you can share recipes, tips, and photos of your creations.

05

DOCUMENT YOUR JOURNEY

Keep a cooking journal or start a blog documenting your culinary adventures. It is a fun way to keep track of what you've made and allows you to reflect on your progress and share your experiences with others.

I have a good friend named Emma who decided to explore baking after retiring and started with simple cookies and cakes. Soon, she was baking elaborate pastries and artisan breads. Emma joined an online baking community where she shared her successes (and occasional flops), learned new techniques, and made friends who shared her passion. Now, her home is known as the go-to place for delicious baked goods!

MAKING THE MOST OF YOUR TIME AT HOME

Your home is filled with opportunities for joy, creativity, and fulfillment. By staying active and engaged, you can transform every day into a delightful adventure. Whether you're discovering new hobbies, researching creative projects, or simply enjoying the little things, there's always something extraordinary to explore.

Embrace the freedom that retirement brings. Try new activities, experiment with different projects, and allow yourself the pleasure of pursuing your interests. From cooking and gardening to woodworking and photography, each new endeavor adds a splash of color to your life and keeps your mind and body vibrant.

Finding fulfillment and joy in home-based activities is about the journey. Enjoy the process, celebrate your successes, and don't be afraid to laugh at the occasional misstep. Every moment spent exploring your passions is a step towards a richer, more satisfying retirement.

So, roll up your sleeves, jump right into those projects, and *let your home be the canvas* for your creativity and joy.

Here's to making every day a new adventure right in the comfort of your own home. Happy exploring!

CHAPTER FOUR

HEALTHCARE HIJINKS

Navigating the Medical Maze

Trust me, I know what you're thinking, but maintaining your health in retirement doesn't have to be a chore. In fact, it can be one of the most enjoyable and fulfilling parts of this new chapter in your life. Imagine waking up each day feeling energized and ready to dive into activities that keep you both happy and healthy.

But let's be honest - the world of healthcare can feel like a bit of a maze. Maybe you're scratching your head over Medicare plans, feeling a bit uneasy about potential health issues, or struggling to find the motivation to stay active now that you don't have a daily routine pulling you out of bed. These are common concerns, and you're certainly not alone. The good news? This chapter is here to help you navigate those confusing healthcare options and turn health maintenance into something you look forward to rather than dread.

Think of this chapter as your guide to making the most of the healthcare options available while also finding joy in healthy activities that fit seamlessly into your daily life. We will explore how to take charge of your health, from understanding your healthcare choices to discovering fun and motivating ways to stay physically active. It doesn't matter if you are trying a new sport, joining a fitness class, or simply making healthier eating choices;

there are countless ways to keep your body and mind in *tip-top shape.*

So, let's set aside those worries and embrace the journey ahead. With a little knowledge and a lot of enthusiasm, maintaining your health in retirement can be as enjoyable as your favorite hobby. Ready to feel great and live your best life? Let's get to it!

Understanding Your Healthcare Options

Making your way through the world of healthcare can sometimes feel like trying to find your way through a corn maze with a blindfold on - confusing, overwhelming, and more than a little frustrating. But don't worry! With a bit of guidance, you'll find that understanding your healthcare options is not only manageable but also empowering. Whether in the U.S., Canada, Australia, or Great Britain, having a good grasp of your healthcare choices is one of the keys to enjoying a healthy and fulfilling retirement.

In the U.S., Medicare is the big player in healthcare for retirees. If you're 65 or older, you're likely eligible for Medicare, which offers different parts to cover hospital stays (Part A), medical services (Part B), and even prescription drugs (Part D). There's also Medicare Advantage (Part C), which is offered through private insurance companies and combines Parts A and B, often including additional benefits like dental and vision care. Understanding these options and knowing what's covered is essential to ensure you get the care you need without any surprise bills.

But Medicare isn't the only option. You might also consider private insurance plans, either as a supplement to Medicare (like Medigap) or as an alternative. Private insurance can be tailored to your specific needs, but it's important to compare plans carefully, considering factors like premiums, out-of-pocket costs, and what's included in the coverage.

If you're in Canada, you're in luck with a publicly funded healthcare system that covers most medical services. However, you might still want to consider private insurance for things like dental, vision, or prescription drugs that aren't fully covered by the public plan. Similarly, Australia offers Medicare, a public healthcare system providing residents free or low-cost medical services. Like in Canada, many Australians opt for private health insurance to cover additional services or to have more flexibility in choosing healthcare providers.

In Great Britain, the National Health Service (NHS) is your go-to for healthcare, offering a wide range of services free at the point of use. However, private insurance is available for those who want faster access to specialists or elective procedures. Understanding what the NHS covers and when private insurance might be beneficial can help you make better decisions about your healthcare.

No matter where you live, *regular check-ups and preventive care* are your best friends in maintaining good health.

Scheduling annual physicals, routine screenings, and staying on top of vaccinations can catch potential issues early, making them easier to treat. Preventive care isn't just about doctor visits, though—it's about embracing a lifestyle that keeps you healthy. This means eating well, staying active, and managing stress.

When selecting the right healthcare plan, start by assessing your needs. Do you have chronic conditions that require regular care? Are you taking prescription medications? Do you prefer having access to a vast network of doctors, or are you content with a more limited choice if it means lower costs? Once you've identified your priorities, use resources like government websites (Medicare.gov in the U.S., NHS.uk in the U.K., etc.) to compare plans. Many countries also offer free counseling services or workshops to help you understand your options. Don't hesitate to take advantage of these resources—they help you make the best decision for your health.

I heard through the grapevine about a man who, after retiring, found himself overwhelmed by the maze of healthcare options. Unsure of where to begin, he decided to attend a local Medicare workshop. Not only did he leave with a clear understanding of his choices, but he also discovered that his ideal plan was one he hadn't even considered before. That peace of mind was invaluable, allowing him to focus on the more enjoyable aspects of retirement. Like finally taking up that photography hobby he'd been putting off for years.

Staying informed about your healthcare choices and taking an active role in managing your health is one of the most important things you can do in retirement. The peace of mind that comes with knowing you've made informed decisions about your healthcare is priceless. Understanding your options frees up your time and energy to focus on the fun stuff—like trying out those new hobbies and activities we've been discussing!

So, take a deep breath, do a little research, and get those check-ups *on the calendar.*

Your future self will thank you for it! With the right healthcare plan in place and a commitment to preventive care, you're all set to enjoy a long, healthy, and joyful retirement.

ACTIVITIES FOR A HEALTHY LIFESTYLE

Now that you have a solid understanding of your healthcare options, it's time to focus on the exciting ways to keep your body and mind in tip-top shape. Staying healthy doesn't have to be a chore; it can be downright enjoyable. Imagine exploring new sports, whipping up delicious (and nutritious) meals, and even finding joy in the little things like a daily walk through the park.

Up next, we will explore some activities that help you stay fit and healthy and bring a big smile to your face. If you want to try a new sport, join a fun fitness class, or discover the joy of cooking healthy meals, we have something for everyone. And don't worry - we will make sure you stay motivated and inspired every step of the way.

So, lace up those sneakers, grab your yoga mat, and get ready to leap into *a world of health and happiness.*

After all, retirement is the perfect time to explore new activities, challenge yourself, and, most importantly, have fun while doing it!

1. Healthy Eating
Savor the Goodness

Let's talk about one of life's greatest pleasures - eating! But here's the secret - eating well doesn't just tickle your taste buds; it's also the foundation of a healthy, vibrant life. A balanced diet is like giving your body the VIP treatment it deserves, ensuring you feel energized, strong, and ready to take on all the adventures retirement offers.

So, what exactly is a balanced diet? Picture your plate as a colorful palette filled with a variety of foods, with fruits and veggies taking up half of your plate, bringing a rainbow of vitamins, minerals, and fiber. Then there are whole grains, like brown rice and oats, which keep your energy levels steady and your heart happy. And let's not forget the protein - lean meats, fish, beans, or tofu - essential for muscle maintenance, especially as we age. A sprinkle of healthy fats from sources like olive oil, nuts, and avocados rounds out the perfect plate.

> ## But healthy eating isn't just about what's on your plate - it's also about *making smart choices* throughout the day.

Start by keeping your pantry stocked with wholesome snacks, like nuts, seeds, and fresh fruit, so you're never tempted by less nutritious options. And when it comes to mealtime, aim to cook at home more often - this way, you know exactly what's going into your food, and you can control portions and ingredients.

2. Healthy Cooking
Bring Some Fun into the Kitchen

Ready to spice up your kitchen adventures? Healthy cooking is not just about making nutritious meals - it's about turning your kitchen into a playground of flavors, creativity, and pure joy. Whether you're a seasoned chef or just starting out, cooking healthy meals can be one of the most rewarding and delicious parts of your day.

> ## So, let's grab those aprons and dive into the world of healthy, tasty, and downright *delightful cooking*!

First things first - why not join a cooking class? It doesn't matter if they are in-person or online; cooking classes are a great way to learn new skills, discover fresh recipes, and maybe even make a few new friends along the way. If you prefer a social setting, look for local community centers or cooking schools that offer classes focused on healthy meals. There are plenty of online options for those who enjoy learning from the comfort of home. Platforms like "Udemy" and "MasterClass" offer a wide range of courses where you can learn everything from the basics to gourmet healthy cooking, all at your own pace.

But why stop there? The Internet is brimming with resources to help you turn your kitchen into a healthy haven. YouTube channels like "Tasty" are filled with quick, easy, and nutritious recipes that will have you whipping up healthy meals in no time. And if you're looking for a bit more guidance from a seasoned pro, tune into Jamie Oliver's healthy cooking series. His down-to-earth approach and passion for good food make cooking a delightful experience, even if you're just starting out.

Healthy cooking is all about discovering new flavors, experimenting with fresh ingredients, and finding joy in the process. Try swapping out traditional ingredients for healthier alternatives - think zucchini noodles instead of pasta or Greek yogurt instead of sour cream. Not only will you be doing your body a favor, but you'll also discover just how delicious healthy eating can be.

So, if you're sautéing, roasting, or blending, remember that cooking is an adventure. Each meal is an opportunity to nourish your body and delight your senses. Get creative, have fun, and enjoy the satisfaction of knowing that you're making healthy choices, one delicious dish at a time.

Need a little help staying on track? There are some fantastic resources out there to guide you. YouTube channels like "NutritionFacts.org" offer bite-sized videos packed with science-backed tips on healthy eating. Or, if you're a fan of tracking your meals and staying motivated, apps like MyFitnessPal can be your best friend. These tools make it easy to log your meals, monitor your nutritional intake, and even discover new healthy recipes.

3. Finding the Sport That Suits You
Get Moving and Have Fun!

When it comes to staying active, the most important thing is finding a sport that makes you smile - because, let's face it, exercise should be fun! If you want to relive your glory days on the tennis court, try something new like pickleball, or just enjoy a leisurely swim, there's a sport out there that's perfect for you.

So, let's explore
the wonderful world of sports
and find the one that *suits you best*!

First off, think about what you enjoy. Do you love being outdoors, or do you prefer indoor activities? Are you someone who thrives on competition, or do you lean towards more relaxed, solo pursuits? Your answers will help guide you toward the right sport. For example, hiking or golf might be your perfect match if you love nature. Team sports like volleyball or bowling could be a great fit if you enjoy socializing. And if you're all about low-impact exercises, swimming or yoga might be just what you're looking for.

Next, consider your physical abilities and lifestyle. Choosing a sport that feels good for your body and fits into your daily routine is important. If you're just starting out or have specific health considerations, opt for gentler activities like tai chi or water aerobics. These sports are easy on the joints and great for maintaining flexibility and balance. On the other hand, if you're looking for something a bit more vigorous, you might enjoy cycling, tennis, or even dance classes.

To get started, check out your local community centers and sports clubs - they often offer a variety of classes and activities tailored to different interests and fitness levels. These are great places to meet new people and try different sports without making a big commitment. You can also explore online platforms like Meetup.com, where you can find local sports groups and events in your area. Many of these groups welcome beginners and provide a supportive environment to learn and grow.

And don't forget about online resources! Websites and YouTube channels offer tutorials and virtual classes for everything from yoga to martial arts, so you can try out different sports from the comfort of your home before jumping in.

4. Exercising
Developing a Routine That Sticks

Alright, let's get moving! Developing a regular exercise routine is like giving your body a daily dose of happiness. Not only does it keep you fit and healthy, but it also boosts your mood, sharpens your mind, and gives you that extra pep in your step. The best part? Once you find a routine that works for you, it becomes less of a chore and more of a joyful habit.

I met a wonderful woman at the gym who decided to start working with a personal trainer twice a week. She wasn't looking to become a bodybuilder—just to improve her overall health and stay active. The results? Simply amazing! She managed to lower her blood pressure, increase her muscle mass, and improve her balance. But the best part, she told me with a big smile, was being able to run around with her grandkids without getting tired. Her commitment to regular exercise transformed her health and brought her closer to the things she loves most in life.

The first step in building a routine is setting realistic goals. Don't worry—you don't need to train for a marathon (unless you want to!). Start small and think about what you want to achieve. Maybe it's walking 10,000 steps a day, doing yoga three times a week, or simply moving your body for 20 minutes each morning. Whatever your goal, make sure it's something that excites you and feels achievable.

Once you've set your goals, it's time to make a plan. Look at your schedule and find the best time of day for your workouts. Are you a morning person who loves the sunrise, or do you prefer evening strolls? Pick a time that works for you and stick to it—consistency is key to forming a lasting habit.

To keep on track, consider using a fitness app like "7 Minute Workout" or "MyFitnessPal." These apps can help you log your activities, track your progress, and even remind you to get moving. If you prefer more guidance, YouTube fitness channels like "Fitness Blender" offer free workouts ranging from gentle stretches to high-intensity cardio, all designed to fit your schedule.

Sticking to an exercise routine is easier when you *mix things up* and *keep it fun.*

Try different activities to see what you enjoy most—dancing, swimming, or even a bit of strength training. Remember, variety is the spice of life, and the same goes for exercise!

And here's a little secret: don't be too hard on yourself if you miss a day. Life happens, and the important thing is to get back on track without guilt. Celebrate your progress, no matter how small, and keep moving forward.

5. Joining Fitness Classes
Move, Groove, and Make New Friends

Joining fitness classes is a fabulous way to stay active and energized. It doesn't matter if your preference is yoga, Pilates, or even a sassy dance class—these activities are fantastic for your body and mind, helping you feel stronger and healthier every day.

Imagine starting your day with a gentle yoga session, stretching, and breathing your way to tranquility. Not only does yoga improve flexibility and balance, but it's also an excellent way to calm the mind and relieve stress. If you're looking for a fantastic online option, check out "Yoga with Adriene" on YouTube. Adriene's warm, welcoming style makes yoga accessible and fun, no matter your level of experience.

If you're more in the mood to shimmy and shake, why not try a dance class? Dancing is a joyful way to get your heart pumping, boost your mood, and unleash your inner rhythm. Whether it's a lively salsa or a graceful ballroom, dancing brings a smile to your face and a spring to your step. For an online option, "The Ballet Coach" on YouTube offers free ballet classes that are both elegant and energizing—perfect for getting in touch with your inner dancer!

Local community centers and gyms are great places to find fitness classes that suit your style. Many offer everything from Pilates to Zumba, so you can try different classes until you find the one that makes you feel fantastic. And if you prefer staying home, online classes via Zoom or pre-recorded videos allow you to join in the fun from your living room.

So, don't be shy—step into a fitness class, move your body, and *enjoy the benefits of staying active.*

Fitness classes are all about feeling good and keeping your body in top shape!

6. Group Sports
Fun, Fitness, and Friendship

Engaging in group sports or activities like tennis, golf, or team sports is not only a fantastic way to stay fit but also a wonderful opportunity to socialize, laugh, and maybe even spark a bit of friendly competition. You could be hitting the tennis court, swinging a golf club, joining a local softball team, or playing sports with others, which brings a whole new level of fun and camaraderie.

Group sports offer a fun mix of *physical exercise and social interaction.*

Imagine a sunny afternoon spent on the golf course, chatting with friends between swings, or a lively tennis match that gets your heart racing and your spirits soaring. The shared experience of playing together fosters connection, boosts motivation, and adds a dose of joy to your fitness routine.

If you're wondering where to find your sporty tribe, start by checking out local sports leagues and community clubs. Many towns and cities have clubs dedicated to everything from pickleball to bowling. Community centers, YMCAs, and local gyms often organize group sports activities, so you can easily find something that matches your interests and fitness level.

For those who prefer a more modern approach, online platforms like Meetup.com are fantastic for finding sports groups in your area. If you choose to look into a weekend hiking club, a casual soccer league, or a neighborhood golf group, these platforms make it easy to connect with like-minded people who enjoy staying active.

7. Lifting Weights
Pump Up Your Strength and Confidence

Who says weightlifting is just for the young and buff? Lifting weights is a fantastic way to build strength, boost energy, and improve overall physical health, regardless of age. In fact, it's especially important for seniors, helping to maintain muscle mass, bone density, and balance, all of which are key to staying active and independent.

Getting started with weightlifting doesn't mean you must dive into heavy-duty bench presses or powerlifting. The beauty of strength training is that you can start small and work your way up at your own pace. Begin with light weights, like a pair of dumbbells or resistance bands, and focus on exercises targeting major muscle groups—think squats, leg lifts, and shoulder presses. The goal is to build up strength gradually, so there's no rush to add more weight until you're comfortable and confident.

As you get stronger, you can slowly increase the weight and add more repetitions to your routine. The key is consistency—make weightlifting a regular part of your fitness routine, aiming for a few weekly sessions. Not only will you notice improvements in your strength, but you'll also likely feel more energized and confident in your daily activities.

Need a little guidance? Online resources like YouTube are a goldmine for senior-friendly strength training tutorials. Channels like "HASfit" offer easy-to-follow workouts designed specifically for older adults, with plenty of modifications to suit different fitness levels. If you prefer an app, try "FitOn" or "MyFitnessPal," which provide personalized workout plans and track your progress over time.

Let's grab those weights and start lifting! It's not just about building muscles—it's about building a stronger, healthier, and more confident you.

8. Creating a Training Plan
Your Roadmap to Fitness Success

Ready to take your fitness journey to the next level? Creating a personalized training plan is like having a roadmap that guides you toward your goals, keeps you motivated, and ensures that you're making steady progress. Plus, it's a fun way to add structure to your workouts, so you always know exactly what you're doing and why you're doing it.

The beauty of a training plan is that it's tailored just for you. If you aim to build strength, improve your endurance, or simply stay active, having a plan helps you stay consistent and focused. For example, suppose you're a fan of walking. In that case, your plan might include gradually increasing your distance and pace, with a few strength-training sessions sprinkled in for good measure. Or, if you're just starting out, a gentle routine that mixes stretching, light weights, and low-impact cardio might be your perfect fit.

Creating your own plan
doesn't have to be complicated.

Start by setting clear, achievable goals—whether it's walking 30 minutes a day, doing yoga three times a week, or working up to a 5K run. Then, break down those goals into weekly and daily activities. Mix it up with different exercises to keep things interesting, and don't forget to schedule rest days to give your body time to recover.

Need some inspiration? Fitness apps like "FitOn" and "C25K" offer customizable workout plans that cater to all levels, from beginners to seasoned fitness enthusiasts. These apps can help you track your progress, adjust your plan as you improve, and even throw in a few motivational pep talks along the way.

9. Daily Walk

Step Into Wellness, One Stroll at a Time

Let's take a walk, shall we? There's something wonderfully simple yet incredibly powerful about making a daily walk part of your routine. It's more than just putting one foot in front of the other—it's about boosting your cardiovascular health, melting away stress, and soaking up the beauty of the world around you. Additionally, it's an easy, low-impact way to stay active and keep those muscles and joints happy.

The benefits of a daily walk *are endless.*

It gets your heart pumping and improves circulation, but also clears your mind and lifts your spirits. Imagine starting your day with a peaceful morning stroll, the fresh air filling your lungs as you greet the day. Or perhaps you prefer an evening walk, unwinding after dinner as the sun sets. Whenever you choose to walk, it's a chance to connect with nature, reflect on your thoughts, and simply enjoy the moment.

Incorporating walking into your daily routine is easier than you might think. Try taking a walk after meals—it's a great way to aid digestion and sneak in some extra steps. If you're feeling adventurous, explore local parks, trails, or perhaps your neighborhood. Each walk can be a mini-adventure, discovering new paths and sights.

To make your walks even more enjoyable and keep track of your progress, consider using apps like "Pacer" or "Map My Walk." These handy tools let you set goals, track your distance, and compare your walks over time. You might be surprised at how quickly those steps add up!

HEALTHY, HAPPY, AND THRIVING
EMBRACING HEALTH AND WELLNESS IN RETIREMENT

Congratulations, you're on your way to making health and wellness one of the best parts of your retirement journey! Maintaining your well-being is not just about staying fit—it's about embracing the joy of feeling strong, active, and full of life. Whether you're whipping up healthy meals, joining a fun fitness class, or simply taking a daily walk, each step towards a healthier lifestyle brings more energy, happiness, and fulfillment to your golden years.

Remember, retirement is your time to shine, and taking care of your health is the key to enjoying every moment to the fullest. The activities we've explored together aren't just good for you—they're also fun, engaging, and a great way to discover new passions. By prioritizing wellness, you're setting yourself up for a vibrant and satisfying retirement filled with adventures, laughter, and plenty of feel-good moments.

So, keep moving, smiling, and, most importantly, *embracing the incredible journey* of health and wellness. Here's to a retirement that's *lived and lived well*!

CHAPTER FIVE

MENTAL GYMNASTICS

Keeping Your Brain Active

The world is your oyster, and your mind is your most valuable pearl! As we step into this exciting new stage of life, keeping our brains sharp and active is just as important as staying physically fit.

After all, a *healthy mind* is the key to enjoying *all the adventures* retirement offers.

Let's be honest—many of us worry about cognitive decline as we age. The thought of forgetting names, misplacing keys, or feeling mentally sluggish can be unsettling. But here's the good news: your brain is like a muscle; just like any muscle, it gets stronger the more you use it. By keeping your mind engaged and stimulated, you can maintain your mental sharpness, improve memory, boost creativity, and reduce the risk of cognitive decline.

Retirement is the perfect time to embrace mental activity with open arms. With the hustle and bustle of your working years behind you, you now have the freedom to explore new interests, dive into challenging activities, and learn skills you've always wanted to master. The possibilities are endless, whether it's picking up a new hobby, solving puzzles, or even writing that book you've always dreamed of.

So, let's set out on this joyful journey of lifelong learning and mental fitness together. This chapter is packed with fun, engaging activities and practical tips to keep your brain buzzing with excitement. Remember, a sharp mind isn't just about preventing decline—it's about thriving, discovering new passions, and making the most of every moment in this exciting stage of life. Get ready to flex those mental muscles and enjoy every moment!

Why Mental Stimulation is Important in Retirement

You've spent years sharpening your mind through work, socializing, and learning new skills. Now, in retirement, it's time to keep that momentum going. Just like your muscles need regular exercise to stay strong, your brain needs mental workouts to stay sharp. But don't worry—keeping your brain active isn't just good for you; it's also fun, fulfilling, and a great way to add more joy to your later years.

I recently caught up with an old childhood friend, Caroline, who always had a sharp mind and a love for learning. Even now, in retirement, she's the same. Caroline told me about how she joined a local book club and started taking up chess, something she hadn't played since we were kids. Not only has she rekindled her love for these activities, but she's also noticed how much sharper and more engaged she feels every day. Caroline swears that these mental challenges have kept her memory strong and her days filled with excitement and purpose.

| Let's start with the science:

Research shows that engaging in mental activities can significantly reduce the risk of cognitive decline. A study published in the journal Neurology found that adults who regularly participated in mentally stimulating activities, like reading or playing games, had a slower rate of memory decline than those who didn't. Another study from the Alzheimer's Association found that people who frequently challenge their brains through learning and problem-solving activities are less likely to develop Alzheimer's disease and other forms of dementia.

So, what's going on in your brain when you tackle a crossword puzzle, learn a new language, or even take up knitting? These activities create new neural connections and strengthen existing ones, like physical exercise builds muscle. This process, known as neuroplasticity, is your brain's ability to adapt and change throughout your life. Keeping your mind engaged gives your brain a workout, which helps improve memory, problem-solving skills, and overall cognitive function.

But the benefits of mental stimulation go beyond just keeping your memory sharp. Staying mentally active also contributes to your overall well-being. When you immerse yourself in a challenging task, your brain releases feel-good chemicals like dopamine, which boost your mood and reduce stress. You could be reveling in the satisfaction of completing a jigsaw puzzle or the joy of mastering a new recipe. These activities help you stay positive and mentally resilient.

Mental stimulation also plays a crucial role in combating loneliness and isolation, two common challenges in retirement. Engaging in mentally stimulating activities often involves social interaction, a critical factor in maintaining mental health. Joining a book club, participating in a trivia night, or simply sharing your latest project with a friend can create meaningful connections and keep loneliness at bay.

Socializing isn't just about keeping company; it's about *engaging your brain* in conversations, debates, and shared experiences.

A study from the University of Michigan found that social interaction can enhance cognitive function and even improve your ability to solve problems. So, by staying mentally active and socially engaged, you're giving your brain double the benefits.

Moreover, mental activities give you a sense of purpose and accomplishment, which is essential for a fulfilling retirement. Learning a new skill or hobby isn't just about the activity itself—it's about the confidence and pride you feel as you progress and achieve your goals. This sense of purpose can significantly enhance your quality of life, making each day more meaningful and enjoyable.

Keeping your brain active in retirement isn't just a nice-to-have; it's a must-do for maintaining your cognitive health and overall happiness. The more you engage in mentally stimulating activities, the better equipped you'll be to enjoy this exciting phase of life. So, if you decide to dive into a good book, explore a new hobby, or join a community group, remember that you're not just having fun—you're also giving your brain the workout it needs to stay sharp, happy, and healthy.

Tips and Strategies to Boost Your Mental Fitness

Alright, let's look into the nuts and bolts of keeping that brilliant brain of yours in top shape! We've talked about the importance of mental stimulation and how it can help you stay sharp, happy, and engaged throughout retirement. Now, it's time to get practical with some easy-to-follow tips and strategies to make mental fitness a fun and exciting part of your daily routine.

Think of this as your mental fitness plan—a joyful blend of activities, tools, and social connections that will keep your mind buzzing with excitement. Whether you're a fan of puzzles, a lover of books, or someone who thrives on learning new skills, there's something here for everyone. And the best part? These activities are great for your brain and also a lot of fun!

Routines for Mental Activities: Making Brain Workouts a Daily Delight.

Let's discuss turning your mental fitness into a joyful, regular part of your life. Just like your morning coffee or afternoon stroll, keeping your brain active can be a fun habit that seamlessly fits into your daily or weekly routine. The trick? Consistency and a little bit of planning.

First, let's start with the idea of setting aside dedicated time for your brain workouts. Think of this time as a gift to yourself—a few moments in your day when you can focus on keeping your mind sharp and engaged. It doesn't matter if it's ten minutes with a crossword puzzle over breakfast or an hour in the evening to dive into a good book; finding time that works for you is vital. The important part is to make it a regular habit so your brain knows it's time to get a little exercise.

Now, to keep things interesting, variety is your best friend. Just like mixing up your physical workouts to target different muscle groups, you'll want to balance different types of mental activities. Reading, for example, is fantastic for expanding your vocabulary and keeping your mind curious. But how about adding some puzzles or brain games to challenge your problem-solving skills? Or maybe it's time to finally learn that new language you've been curious about—there's no better way to keep those neurons firing on all cylinders!

Try scheduling specific activities for certain days to make your routine more effective. Maybe Mondays are for tackling brain teasers, Wednesdays are dedicated to reading something new, and Fridays are all about learning a new skill or hobby. This way, you keep things fresh, and your brain gets a well-rounded workout.

Remember, the goal is to enjoy these activities, not to make them feel like a chore. By integrating a variety of mental exercises into your routine, you'll keep your mind sharp and add a touch of joy and fulfillment to your days. So, go ahead—schedule that "me time" for your brain, and watch how quickly it becomes a highlight of your week!

Resources and Tools: Your Brain's New Best Friends.

Ready to give your brain a boost? Thanks to the wonders of technology and the wealth of knowledge out there, keeping your mind sharp has never been easier—or more fun! If you're a fan of reading, love solving puzzles, or are eager to learn new skills, there's a resource just waiting to help you on your mental fitness journey.

First up, let's talk apps. Lumosity and Elevate are two fantastic brain-training apps that offer a variety of games designed to challenge your memory, focus, and problem-solving skills. These apps make mental workouts feel like play, with daily exercises that adapt to your performance level, ensuring you're constantly improving. Spend just 10 minutes a day on these apps, and you'll be amazed at how much sharper you feel over time. Plus, the friendly competition with yourself can be very addictive!

If you're more of a reader, there are plenty of books out there that will not only entertain but also stimulate your mind. "The Brain Fitness Book" by Rita Carter is a great pick, offering tips and exercises to keep your brain healthy and engaged. For a deep dive into how the brain works and how to keep it sharp, try "Keep Sharp" by Dr. Sanjay Gupta—it's packed with science-based strategies for maintaining cognitive health. And for something a bit more playful, "Einstein's Riddle" by Jeremy Stangroom is filled with puzzles and brainteasers that will challenge you to think outside the box.

Looking to mix things up with some online resources? Websites like BrainBashers and Braingle offer a ton of puzzles, quizzes, and games that cater to all levels of difficulty. These sites are perfect for a quick mental pick-me-up during your day, and you can even challenge friends or family to join in the fun.

Finally, don't forget about the wonders of podcasts and audiobooks. Listening to thought-provoking content while on a walk or doing chores is a great way to keep your brain engaged. Apps like Audible offer a vast library of audiobooks on everything from history and science to fiction and self-improvement. Meanwhile, podcasts like "TED Talks Daily" or "Stuff You Should Know" cover fascinating topics that will pique your curiosity.

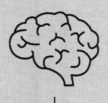

ACTIVITIES FOR KEEPING YOUR BRAIN ACTIVE

Ready to have some fun while giving your brain a good workout? This section is all about keeping your mind sharp, curious, and full of life with activities that are as enjoyable as they are beneficial. From brain-training apps to exploring new hobbies, we've got a whole buffet of mental exercises to keep your cognitive gears turning and your spirits high. It makes no difference if you're a tech enthusiast, a puzzle lover, or someone who's always eager to learn something new; there's something here for everyone. So, let's get going and discover the joy of keeping your brain active and engaged!

1. Train Your Mind with Apps

Ready to turn your smartphone or tablet into a brain-boosting machine? Brain training apps like „Lumosity", „Peak", and „Elevate" are here to make mental fitness both fun and effective. These apps are packed with games and exercises designed to challenge your memory, sharpen your focus, and enhance your problem-solving skills—all while feeling like you're just having a bit of fun. Spend just a few minutes a day playing these games, and you'll soon notice your brain getting quicker and more agile.

With new challenges every day,
you'll never get bored.
It's like having a *personal trainer*
for your mind right in your pocket!

2. Mind Training with Games and Exercises

Who says keeping your mind sharp can't be a blast? Brain games like crosswords, Sudoku, and chess are a fun way to pass the time and a powerful tool for maintaining cognitive function. These games are perfect for challenging your brain to think critically, solve problems, and keep those neurons firing. Picture this: solving a crossword over your morning coffee to jump-start your brain, tackling a Sudoku puzzle during lunch to keep your mind active, or playing a quick game of chess online in the evening to unwind. Each activity provides a specific mental challenge, and incorporating them into your daily routine can significantly benefit your cognitive health.

It's all about *finding joy* in these small, stimulating exercises culminating in a big win for your brain!

Unlock your free puzzle collection!

Get access to our free collection of Sudoku, word searches, and crosswords —perfect for keeping your brain sharp and having some fun at the same time.

SIMPLY **SCAN THE QR-CODE,** DOWNLOAD YOUR PUZZLES AND START SOLVING RIGHT AWAY!

3. Reading

Let's dive into the wonderful world of reading—one of the best ways to keep your mind buzzing with activity! Whether you're flipping through a thrilling novel, exploring a fascinating article, or immersing yourself in a thought-provoking blog, reading engages your brain, improves memory, expands your vocabulary, and hones critical thinking skills.

The beauty of reading is that there's always something new to discover. So, *mix it up!*

From books and magazines to online articles and research papers, keeping various materials in your reading list will ensure your mind stays sharp, curious, and always ready for the next adventure.

4. Writing a Book

Have you ever considered the magic of putting pen to paper or fingers to keyboard? Writing isn't just about words—it's about giving your thoughts and imagination a playground where anything is possible. Whether you're jotting down your daily reflections in a journal, spinning short stories that capture little slices of life, or finally diving into that novel you've always wanted to write, writing has incredible benefits for your mind.

Let's get specific: Journaling can be a fantastic way to start. Set aside a few quiet moments daily to capture your thoughts, feelings, and observations. It's not about perfect grammar or crafting a masterpiece; it's about letting your mind wander freely and putting those wandering thoughts into words. This simple practice sharpens your critical thinking and helps you process emotions and experiences, making sense of the world around you.

If storytelling is more your style, why not create your own short stories? Start with a single idea—maybe a memory from childhood, a dream you had, or even a "what if" scenario that's been tickling your brain. From there, let your imagination take over. The beauty of short stories is that they allow you to explore different perspectives and genres without the commitment of a full-length novel. It's a great way to experiment with style and voice while giving your brain a workout in creativity and problem-solving.

And speaking of novels, if you've always had a book inside you, now's the time to let it out. Start by outlining your ideas—who your characters are, what the plot is, and where it all unfolds. Don't worry about making it perfect right away. The key is writing regularly setting aside specific weekly times to add to your story. Before you know it, those pages will add up, and you'll see your vision taking shape. Not only will this challenge your mind in new ways, but it could also lead to the satisfaction of holding a finished book in your hands.

Remember, the goal of writing isn't just to produce something tangible; it's also about *the joy of the process.*

Whether you're writing for yourself or others, each word you put down is a step towards keeping your brain sharp, your creativity flowing, and your emotions in balance. So, grab that pen or open that laptop—your mind will thank you for the adventure, and who knows? You might just uncover a talent you never knew you had!

5. Research Your Family Tree

Take a trip down memory lane and discover the stories hidden in your family history! Researching your genealogy and building a family tree isn't just a hobby—it's an exciting way to keep your brain actively engaged, offering a rich blend of research, critical thinking, and a dash of detective work. This educational adventure brings your personal history to life, providing both mental stimulation and a profound connection to your roots.

Plus, you might stumble upon some *fun surprises* and *memorable stories* to share at the next family gathering!

To get started, consider using resources like Ancestry.com, one of the most comprehensive platforms for genealogy research. This website provides access to a wide variety of records, including birth, marriage, and death certificates, as well as census data and military records. Simply start by entering the names of your parents or grandparents, and watch as the site's algorithms begin to connect the dots. It's like watching a puzzle come together, one piece at a time.

If you prefer a more hands-on approach, visit local libraries or historical societies to explore physical archives, old newspapers, and public records. Many libraries offer access to genealogy-specific resources, such as HeritageQuest or FamilySearch, which can be invaluable for deepening your research. These trips to the archives give you a deeper understanding of your family's history and allow you to practice critical thinking as you piece together information from various sources.

Another powerful tool is DNA testing kits, such as those offered by 23andMe or MyHeritage. These kits can provide insights into your ethnic background and connect you with distant relatives you may not have known existed. The results can add new branches to your family tree, giving you a broader view of your ancestry and potentially opening doors to new research opportunities.

As you gather information, be sure to organize it using genealogy software or even a simple spreadsheet. This will help you keep track of dates, relationships, and sources, making it easier to spot patterns and verify connections. Tools like Family Tree Maker or RootsMagic can help you create a visual representation of your family tree, allowing you to see your history unfold before your eyes.

To make the experience even more rewarding, consider documenting your findings in a family history book or digital archive. Share these stories with your relatives—many who may be unaware of their rich heritage. Not only will this deepen your connection to your roots, but it will also create a treasured resource for future generations to come!

6. Explore Creative Arts

Ready to give your brain a workout in the most colorful and expressive way possible? Engaging in creative arts, such as painting, drawing, or crafting, is a fantastic way to keep your mind active while unleashing your inner artist. These activities aren't just about producing beautiful pieces; they also stimulate your brain by encouraging creativity, problem-solving, and fine motor skills. Whether you're experimenting with watercolors, sketching in a journal, or piecing together a mosaic, the process of creating art helps improve focus and reduces stress. Plus, seeing your ideas come to life on canvas or paper is incredibly fulfilling. And here's the best part: you don't need to be a professional artist to reap the benefits—just dive in, get your hands messy, and enjoy the creative flow.

Every stroke of the brush or pencil
is like a *mental stretch,*
keeping your brain flexible, engaged,
and ready for more!

7. Discover New Skills

Ready to surprise your brain with something new?

Learning unexpected skills or hobbies is a fantastic way to *keep your mind sharp and adaptable.*

Whether you decide to pick up a musical instrument, master the art of juggling, or dive into a hands-on craft like pottery or knitting, these activities offer a unique mental workout. Unlike traditional learning, these skills engage different parts of your brain, fostering creativity and problem-solving in exciting new ways. By embracing these fresh twists, you're promoting neuroplasticity—the brain's incredible ability to form new connections and pathways. So, why not surprise yourself? Your brain will love the challenge, and you'll have fun uncovering hidden talents as you go!

8. Embrace Technology

Why let the kids have all the fun with gadgets? Embracing technology is not just for the younger crowd—it's an exciting way to keep your brain buzzing with activity and stay connected in today's fast-paced world. Whether you're learning how to use a new smartphone, mastering video calls on Zoom, or exploring apps that help manage your daily life, diving into the digital world keeps your mind sharp, adaptable, and curious.

Let's start with the basics: if you've got a smartphone, you're already holding a world of possibilities in your hand. Take some time to explore features you might not have tried yet—such as setting up a virtual calendar, organizing your contacts, or using voice commands to send messages or search the web. If you're new to video calls, why not try out Zoom or FaceTime? These platforms are fantastic for staying in touch with loved ones, especially when in-person visits aren't possible. And don't worry if it feels a bit daunting at first. There are plenty of tutorials online that can guide you step by step, or you could even ask a tech-savvy friend or family member for a quick lesson.

Social media is another fun and engaging way to stay connected and mentally active. Platforms like Facebook and Instagram allow you to catch up with friends and family, join interest-based groups, and learn new things through educational pages and videos. If you're feeling adventurous, you might enjoy exploring Pinterest for endless inspiration on hobbies, recipes, and DIY projects. Not only does engaging with social media keep you in the loop, but it also offers a chance to exercise your brain as you navigate new platforms, participate in discussions, and discover fresh content.

Ready to take it a step further? Consider exploring the world of smart home devices. These gadgets, like Amazon's Alexa or Google's Nest Hub, can do everything from playing your favorite music to helping you manage your household with voice commands. Imagine turning off your lights, adjusting the thermostat, or even getting weather updates—all without lifting a finger! Learning to set up and use these devices is practical and a great way to keep your brain engaged with new technology.

If you're feeling incredibly bold, why not dip your toes into the world of coding? While it might sound intimidating, beginner-friendly platforms like Codecademy or Scratch make learning to code fun and accessible. Even a basic understanding of coding can enhance your problem-solving skills and open up a whole new realm of possibilities—creating your own website, automating simple tasks, or just understanding how the technology around you works.

Don't forget about the power of apps to help manage your daily life. From fitness apps that track your steps and remind you to stay active to finance apps that help you budget and manage your money, there's an app for nearly every aspect of your life. Take some time to explore the app store on your smartphone or tablet—you might find tools that simplify tasks, help you stay organized, or even introduce you to new hobbies.

So, go ahead and embrace technology —a vibrant, *ever-expanding playground* for your brain.

Each new tech skill you pick up is a little victory, keeping you connected, engaged, and ready to take on the world in an invigorating and fascinating way. And who knows? You might just discover a new passion along the way!

9. Dive into New Knowledge

Craving something to satisfy your intellectual curiosity? Expanding your horizons by learning something new, like a language, a slice of history, or a scientific concept, keeps your brain engaged and thriving in a different way.

This isn't just about skills —it's about *diving deep into subjects* that spark your interest and keep your mind active.

Take up Spanish, explore the mysteries of ancient civilizations, or immerse yourself in the wonders of astrophysics. Continuous learning of new topics prevents cognitive decline and adds a burst of excitement to your daily life. With online courses, documentaries, and educational podcasts at your fingertips, you can explore a wealth of knowledge right from the comfort of your home. So, pick a topic that excites you, and watch how it ignites your curiosity and joy!

10. Meditation

Let's take a moment to breathe—literally. Meditation is like a soothing balm for your brain, helping to improve focus, reduce stress, and enhance mental clarity.

By practicing mindfulness, you're giving your brain a chance to *relax, reset, and recharge.*

If you're new to meditation, apps like Headspace or Calm offer guided sessions that make it easy to start. Just a few minutes each day can make a world of difference in how you feel and think. So, find a cozy spot, close your eyes, and let your mind unwind—you've earned it!

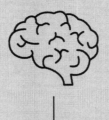

CURIOSITY NEVER RETIRES!

Remember, keeping your brain active is one of the most joyful and rewarding things you can do. From learning new skills to exploring fascinating topics, mental fitness is your ticket to a vibrant, fulfilling life with exciting discoveries and challenges. Think of every day as an opportunity to stretch your mind, spark your curiosity, and embrace the thrill of lifelong learning.

Integrating these activities into your daily routine means you're not only maintaining your cognitive health but enriching your life with purpose, fun, and endless possibilities.

So go ahead,
jump into these mental workouts
with enthusiasm,
and *enjoy the journey*.

After all, your brain deserves to keep dancing with joy, no matter how many candles are on your birthday cake!

CHAPTER SIX

SOCIAL
SHENANIGANS

Staying Connected

Retirement is filled with opportunities for new adventures, fresh beginnings, and, most importantly, the chance to become a social butterfly (or at least a well-connected caterpillar). As we transition into this exciting phase, staying connected with others is not just a nice-to-have; it's a must-have for well-being and happiness. After all, no one wants to be the lone ranger at the retirement rodeo!

Think of social interactions as the sprinkles on the retirement cupcake—they don't just fill your calendar; they sweeten your life. Engaging with others keeps your mind sharp, your emotions balanced, and your heart full. Plus, it's a great excuse to get out of your pajamas before noon (or not, we don't judge).

You see, human beings are wired for connection, like Wi-Fi, but way better. We thrive when we engage with others, share experiences, and create memories together. And now that you're not tied down by the 9-to-5 grind, you've got all the time in the world to choose how you spend your days and, more importantly, who you spend them with.

This is your golden opportunity
to reconnect with old friends,
make new ones,
and *deepen the relationships
that truly matter.*

So go on, dust off that Rolodex (or smartphone), and start making those connections count!

Let me tell you about my brother-in-law, Tom. When he retired, he wasn't quite sure how he would fill his days. But instead of slowing down, he decided to get involved with a local cycling club. What started as a casual interest quickly became a vibrant, thriving social network. Every weekend, Tom would set out with his new group of friends, pedaling through scenic routes and sharing stories along the way. Not only did these rides keep him physically active, but they also gave him a sense of camaraderie and belonging. Now, Tom's calendar is busier than ever, filled with group rides, coffee meetups, and even the occasional weekend getaway with his cycling buddies. His story is a perfect example of how retirement can be the beginning of some of the most rewarding friendships and experiences of your life.

As you set out on this journey, remember that staying socially connected not only helps you to avoid loneliness, but also to embrace the joy that comes from being part of a community. Whether you're rekindling old friendships or forging new ones, retirement offers the perfect stage to enrich your life with meaningful connections. So, get ready to laugh, share, and create new memories with the people who make your life shine!

The Importance of
Social Connections

Staying connected with others is a fundamental aspect of a healthy, fulfilling life. Social connections are like a safety net for both our mental and physical well-being, weaving together threads of companionship, love, and support that lift us up, especially in our golden years.

Science has long shown that humans are *inherently social creatures*.

From the earliest days of human history, our ancestors survived and thrived by sticking together, forming communities, and sharing resources. This need for connection is deeply ingrained in our DNA. Even today, the power of social interactions continues to play a crucial role in our overall health. Numerous studies have highlighted the importance of maintaining strong social ties, particularly as we age.

One study conducted by researchers at Harvard University, part of the famous Harvard Study of Adult Development, followed participants for over 80 years. The findings were clear - the quality of our relationships profoundly impacts our health and happiness. Those who maintained close, meaningful relationships were happier and also lived longer, healthier lives. The study showed that loneliness and isolation could be as harmful to our health as smoking or obesity, leading to increased risks of depression, cognitive decline, and even heart disease.

Another fascinating piece of research comes from a social experiment conducted in the 1970s, known as the "Rat Park" study. In this experiment, scientists observed rats in two different environments— one group was kept in isolated cages with nothing to do. In contrast, the other group lived in a communal environment with plenty of opportunities to play and interact. The results? The rats in the social, enriched environment were far less likely to engage in harmful behaviors, proving that social interactions are essential for mental well-being.

And it's not just rats that benefit from a strong social network! Social support from friends, family, and community can act as a buffer against stress, making coping with life's challenges more manageable. It can also enhance life satisfaction, giving us a sense of purpose and belonging. Regular social interactions help keep our minds sharp, reducing the risk of cognitive decline as we age. In fact, research from the Alzheimer's Association suggests that people who stay socially active are less likely to develop Alzheimer's disease and other forms of dementia.

I heard once about a lady who, after losing her husband, found herself retreating into solitude. Her family became worried as she seemed to be slipping into depression. Then, almost on a whim, she joined a local gardening club. I don't know if this story is true, but it sounds believable. She met a group of like-minded people in the club, and what started as a simple hobby blossomed into deep friendships. She found herself laughing again, looking forward to their weekly meetings and even teaching others about the art of cultivating roses. The transformation was remarkable. Her new social connections brought a renewed sense of joy and vitality to her life, proving just how powerful companionship can be.

Social connections
enrich our lives emotionally
and have tangible benefits
for our physical health.

They provide a sense of community and belonging, offering a vital support system when we need it most. Whether through old friendships or new relationships, staying connected can make all the difference in leading a long, healthy, and fulfilling life.

As you journey through retirement, remember that your relationships are more than just the cherry on top—they're the foundation of a vibrant, happy life. Embrace every opportunity to connect with old friends, family, or new acquaintances, and watch your life become richer, brighter, and more joyful with every shared smile and conversation.

Practical Tips and Strategies
Your Guide to Staying Connected in Retirement

Planning a social life in retirement may take a little effort, but the rewards are totally worth it. Socializing doesn't just happen by magic; it needs a dash of organization to keep the good times rolling.

First up, get yourself a social calendar. Nothing fancy is required—just something to jot down your plans. It could be a simple notebook, a wall calendar, or even a calendar app on your phone. The idea is to have a visual reminder of the fun stuff coming up. Whether it's lunch dates, coffee catch-ups, or group activities, marking them down ensures your schedule stays lively and keeps you connected. Plus, knowing you've got something to look forward to can add a little extra pep to your step!

> ## When it comes to planning activities, *variety is the spice of life.*

For smaller gatherings, think of weekly coffee mornings, cozy game nights, or potluck dinners where everyone brings their favorite dish. These intimate get-togethers are perfect for catching up, sharing stories, and enjoying each other's company in a laid-back setting.

For a bigger splash, consider a monthly or quarterly event. How about a themed dinner party where everyone dresses up and brings a dish from a particular country? Or a backyard barbecue with games and music? You could even organize a group outing to a local theater, museum, or park. These larger events are great for reconnecting with a broader circle of friends and introducing new faces to your social network.

The goal isn't to pack your calendar but to create meaningful, enjoyable experiences that keep you engaged and connected. With a bit of planning, your retirement can be full of laughter, friendship, and unforgettable moments. It's time to grab that calendar and start penciling in the fun—let the good times roll!

Networks and Resources:

With so many networks, clubs, and online platforms at your fingertips, making new friends and finding fun activities is easier than ever. The trick is knowing where to look and what's available to you.

Community centers are a great starting point. These local hubs offer a variety of classes, workshops, and social events, many of which are tailor-made for retirees. Whether it's a weekly art class, a fitness group, or a monthly potluck, community centers are buzzing with activities that help you meet people who share your interests. As an added bonus, they're right in your neighborhood, making it super convenient to pop in and see what's going on.

Local clubs are your go-to if you're passionate about a specific hobby. Many towns have clubs for everything from gardening and photography to book discussions and hiking. Joining one lets you dive deeper into your favorite activities and connects you with a community of like-minded folks. Check local bulletin boards at libraries, cafes, or grocery stores for information on clubs that might interest you.

And let's not forget the digital world! Online platforms like Meetup let you search for groups based on your location and interests—whether it's walking groups, wine-tasting clubs, or even a knitting circle. It's a fun way to explore new activities and meet new friends with just a few clicks.

For those who like a more relaxed approach, Facebook Groups offer a chance to engage with communities on just about any topic. Whether you're into travel, crafts, or local history, there's probably a group out there just waiting for you to join the conversation. You can chat, share experiences, and even plan meetups with members in your area.

Overcoming Social Anxiety:

Jumping into new social situations can feel like taking a plunge into a chilly pool—refreshing but a bit nerve-wracking at first! Social anxiety is normal, especially when you're facing something new, but the good news is that it's totally manageable.

Step one? Acknowledge that it's okay to feel a little nervous. We all have those moments, and that's perfectly fine. The trick is not letting those jitters stop you from enjoying all the connections waiting to be made.

Remember, everyone's probably *just as eager* to connect *as you are* —maybe even a little nervous too!

Start small. Try a smaller gathering or casual one-on-one coffee instead of diving into a big event. It's less overwhelming and a great way to ease into socializing. As you build confidence in these settings, more significant events will start to feel like a breeze.

Preparation is your secret weapon. Before an event, think of a few conversation starters or topics you're comfortable with. Got a hobby you love? A recent funny story? Keep these in mind, and you'll feel more at ease striking up a conversation.

And here's a tip: focus on listening. We often get so caught up in what we'll say next that we forget the power of just being a good listener. Ask questions, show interest, and let the chat flow naturally. People love someone who really listens, and it takes the pressure off you.

Lastly, be kind to yourself. If you're feeling anxious, remember it's okay to go at your own pace. Celebrate small wins, like starting a conversation or attending a new group. Each step builds your confidence, and before you know it, you might just be the life of the party—or at least thoroughly enjoying yourself!

Maintaining Old Connections:

As you jump into the excitement of retirement, it's easy to get swept away by all the new adventures on the horizon. But let's not forget about the golden oldies—the friends and colleagues who've been there through thick and thin. Keeping these connections alive adds a wonderful layer of continuity and joy to your life, and it's easier than you might think.

First things first: make staying in touch a regular thing. No need for grand gestures—a quick phone call can do wonders to brighten your day and theirs. Set up a weekly or monthly check-in with a friend or former colleague, and stick to it. These small, consistent efforts are the glue that keeps those relationships strong, no matter how much time has passed or the distance between you.

For a more personal touch, why not embrace today's tech? Video chats are a brilliant way to see those familiar faces, even if you're miles apart. With Zoom, FaceTime, or WhatsApp, you can catch up over a virtual cup of coffee, all from the comfort of your favorite chair. It's like being there in person, minus the hassle of finding parking!

And, of course, nothing beats a good old-fashioned face-to-face meetup. Whether it's a casual lunch, a weekend getaway, or a simple stroll in the park, spending quality time together can reignite that camaraderie and create new memories.

In the end, keeping those old connections alive is like tending to a garden—you don't need to water it every day, but with a little care, it'll continue to thrive. Make that call, send that message, and cherish the relationships that have been part of your journey. After all, old friends are like a fine wine—they just get better with time.

SOCIAL ADVENTURES:
FUN WAYS TO STAY CONNECTED AND ENGAGED

Staying socially engaged is not just about filling your calendar. It's about filling your life with laughter, love, and shared experiences. Up next, we'll explore a variety of fun and fulfilling activities that will help you stay connected, both with the people you already know and those you've yet to meet. From nurturing lifelong friendships to exploring new interests, these activities are designed to keep your social life vibrant and your heart full.

1. Stay in Touch with Friends

There's nothing quite like the comfort of old friends who've been with you over the years in good times and bad. Make it a habit to reach out regularly. Set a reminder to call or video chat once a week or plan a monthly lunch or coffee date to catch up in person. If distance is an issue, why not start a group chat where you can all share updates, photos, and the occasional joke? Sending a quick "thinking of you" text or a funny meme can brighten someone's day and keep the connection alive.

The key is consistency
—prioritize your friendships,
and they'll continue to enrich your life
with joy and support.

2. Keep in Touch with Former Colleagues

Just because you've hung up your work hat doesn't mean you have to say goodbye to the connections you've built over the years.

Keeping in touch with former colleagues is enjoyable and *keeps your professional network alive.*

Schedule regular lunches or coffee meetups to catch up on life and stay in the loop with industry trends. Consider attending networking events or industry conferences together; it's a great way to stay informed and maintain those valuable connections. You can also share interesting articles or insights via email or LinkedIn to keep the conversation going. By staying connected, you're not just preserving friendships—you're keeping a finger on the pulse of the industry, which can open doors to new opportunities, collaborations, or even just a good chat about the "good old days."

3. Make New Friends

Retirement is the perfect time to expand your social circle and make new friends who share your interests and passions. One of the easiest ways to meet new people is by diving into activities and hobbies you love. Join a local club or group that aligns with your interests—a gardening club, a photography group, or even a wine-tasting society. These settings naturally bring together like-minded individuals, making initiating conversations and forming connections easier.

Don't be shy about *starting conversations* when you're in a new group.

A simple "What got you into this hobby?" or "Have you tried any new activities lately?" can be a great icebreaker. Complimenting someone's work or asking for advice on a shared interest opens the door to deeper discussions. If you're attending a larger event, consider bringing a friend along—it can make stepping into new social circles less intimidating and give you both a chance to meet new people together.

Another tip? Be consistent. Regular attendance at group meetings or activities helps you become a familiar face, making it easier for friendships to develop. And remember, making new friends is all about being open, approachable, and, most importantly, having fun. What are you waiting for? Put yourself out there, embrace the opportunities, and watch your social circle grow in delightful and unexpected ways!

4. Spend Time with Family

Family is like the duct tape of life—it holds everything together, even when things get a little sticky. Spending quality time with them is one of the best investments you can make in retirement, and trust me, the returns are priceless. Whether it's a big family gathering or just a cozy afternoon visit, these moments are what make life sweet and give you stories to laugh about for years to come.

Why not start by setting aside regular days for family time? Maybe it's a weekly Sunday dinner where you pass down secret family recipes (or just order pizza and call it a day). A monthly game night brings out everyone's competitive streak or a spontaneous day trip to the local park where the kids can run wild. The key is to make it a priority and keep it consistent. After all, you don't need a holiday to get the family together—some of the best memories are made on the most ordinary days.

When planning these family shindigs, think about what everyone loves. Is it a backyard picnic with homemade goodies, a baking session with the grandkids where flour ends up everywhere but in the bowl, or a movie marathon that takes you through all the classics? The joy comes from simply being together, so don't stress—just keep it fun and lighthearted.

Here's a little nugget of wisdom: *involve everyone in the planning.*

Let each family member pitch in with ideas or take turns hosting the gatherings. This makes everyone feel included and spices things up with a variety of activities. And if you've spent years working hard and missed out on some of those special moments with the grandkids, now's your time to shine as the fun, wise, slightly mischievous grandparent who's got all the time in the world to spoil them rotten. Get to know them better, share stories, and build those connections that will have them bragging about you to their friends.

5. Get a New Pet

There's nothing quite like the unconditional love and companionship that a pet can bring into your life. For many, especially introverts, a pet becomes more than just a furry friend—it's a loyal companion that fills your home with joy, warmth, and a sense of purpose. Whether you're a dog lover, a cat enthusiast, or someone who enjoys the quiet charm of a small critter, getting a pet can be a life-enhancing decision.

Pets have a magical way of combating loneliness. They're always there, wagging their tails or purring contentedly, reminding you that you're never truly alone. They bring a daily routine, from morning walks to evening snuggles, that gives structure to your day and a reason to get up in the morning with a smile. Plus, who can resist those adorable faces and playful antics?

When choosing a pet, think about what suits your lifestyle. Dogs are fantastic for those who love to stay active, offering plenty of opportunities for walks, playtime, and outdoor adventures. Conversely, cats are perfect if you're looking for a more low-maintenance companion who still provides plenty of affection. If you prefer something smaller, consider a rabbit, guinea pig, or bird—each brings unique charm and companionship.

If you're ready to welcome a pet into your life, consider adopting from a local shelter or rescue organization. Not only will you be giving a loving home to an animal in need, but you'll also find that many shelters offer guidance to help match you with the perfect pet for your lifestyle.

No matter the type of pet you choose, the bond you build will be priceless. Your new friend will brighten your days and bring a sense of fulfillment and joy that's hard to match. Go ahead, open your heart and home to a pet—you'll gain a loyal companion who'll make your retirement years even more wonderful!

6. Teach Others

Have you ever considered joining a group where members teach each other skills and knowledge? It's a fantastic way to share what you know, learn something new, and connect with others who share your curiosity and passion for learning. Imagine the joy of passing on your expertise in gardening while picking up tips on photography or mastering a new recipe from someone else in the group.

It's like a *knowledge exchange* with a generous dose of *fun and friendship* thrown in!

These teaching groups often thrive on the principle that everyone has something valuable to offer. You don't have to be an expert—just willing to share what you know and eager to learn from others. Start by exploring local community centers, libraries, or online platforms like Meetup, where these types of groups often gather. Whether crafting, cooking, or even basic computer skills, there's bound to be a group that matches your interests.

The benefits are twofold: you get to hone your skills, gain new ones, and build meaningful relationships with others who value lifelong learning. Teaching is one of the best ways to reinforce your knowledge, making it a win-win for everyone involved.

7. Get a Part-Time Job

Retirement is all about doing what makes you happy. For some, that includes finding a part-time job that brings a little extra joy, structure, and even some pocket money. A part-time gig isn't just a way to stay busy—it's a fantastic opportunity to meet new people, stay socially active, and keep your skills sharp. Plus, it's a great way to indulge in something you're passionate about without the full-time commitment.

When considering a part-time job, think about what excites you. Do you love being around people? Consider working in a local coffee shop, or bookstore, or even as a tour guide at a museum. If you're handy with tools, offering handyman services or doing odd jobs in your neighborhood could be fulfilling and rewarding. And for animal lovers out there, pet sitting or dog walking can be a delightful way to spend your days.

Another option is to start your own small business, especially if there's a hobby or skill you're passionate about. Dave, a friend from work, always had a knack for woodworking. After retiring, he started making custom furniture and selling it online and at local craft fairs. It didn't take long for word to spread, and now he's busier than ever, doing something he genuinely loves.

If you're unsure where to start, ask around—talk to friends and family, check out local job boards, or explore online job platforms like Indeed or LinkedIn. Sometimes, the best opportunities come from word of mouth, so don't be shy about letting people know you want something to do.

Remember, finding a job that aligns with your interests and passions is key. When you love what you're doing, it doesn't feel like work at all—it's just another way to enjoy life and stay connected with the world around you. Take some time to explore your options, and find that perfect part-time gig that adds a little extra sparkle to your retirement!

8. Online Courses

Why not turn your retirement into a time of endless discovery? Enrolling in online courses is a brilliant way to learn new things and connect with others from the comfort of your own home. With platforms like Coursera, Udemy, or even your local community college, the world's knowledge is literally at your fingertips.

Whether you're interested
in mastering a new language,
diving into the world of photography,
or exploring ancient history,
there's a course out there for you.

Even better is the chance to interact with fellow learners, share ideas, and build a virtual community. Many courses offer discussion boards or group projects, so you're learning and connecting with like-minded individuals who share your curiosity and enthusiasm at the same time. Why not sign up for that course you've always been curious about? It's never too late to learn something new, and you'll be amazed at how it lights up both your mind and spirit!

9. Book Club

If you love to get lost in a good book, why not share that joy with others?

Joining or starting a book club
is a fantastic way
to *dive deeper into literature*
while *meeting regularly*
with fellow book enthusiasts.

The discussions are not limited to plots and characters—they are also about sharing perspectives, sparking intellectual conversations, and enjoying the camaraderie of a great group of friends.

A book club keeps your mind engaged, encourages you to read more, and introduces you to genres and authors you might not have otherwise discovered. Additionally, it's a beautiful excuse to get together, laugh, and even enjoy some snacks!

10. Pet Sitting

Love animals but not ready for the full-time commitment of owning a pet? Pet sitting might just be the perfect solution for you! It's a delightful way to enjoy the companionship of furry friends without the long-term responsibilities. Plus, it's a fantastic option for introverts who cherish quiet, one-on-one time with pets rather than large social gatherings.

Pet sitting allows you to *bond with animals*, experience their *unconditional love*, and even *get a bit of exercise* if you're taking a dog for a walk.

And the best part? You can enjoy all the benefits of pet companionship while maintaining the freedom to travel or keep a flexible schedule. You get the joy of cuddling with a cat or playing with a dog, and when the pet's family returns, you're free to pursue your next adventure.

If you're interested, start by offering your services to friends and family or sign up on pet-sitting platforms like Rover. It's a win-win situation: you help pet owners by caring for their beloved animals, and in return, you get to enjoy the companionship and warmth that pets bring—without the full responsibility of ownership. So become the neighborhood's favorite pet sitter, and let those wagging tails and purring cats bring extra joy to your days!

EMBRACING SOCIAL CONNECTIONS IN RETIREMENT

Staying socially connected in retirement is like giving yourself a gift that keeps on giving. It's not just about packing your calendar with events—it's about filling your life with the warmth of friendships, the fun of shared experiences, and the sheer joy of knowing you're not going through it alone. Social connections are the extra batteries in your retirement remote—keeping the fun going and ensuring you never miss a moment.

As you embark on this new adventure, remember there's a world of opportunities out there just waiting for you. Whether it's joining a book club (where you might actually read the book), volunteering at a local charity, or simply catching up with old friends over a cup of coffee, the key is to stay active and engaged.

Don't hesitate to step out of your comfort zone —a little leap of faith might lead you to the *best friendships you never saw coming.*

And if you ever feel a twinge of nerves, just remember: everyone's looking for connection, and they're probably just as eager to meet someone fabulous—like you!

Retirement is your time to bask in joy, forge new friendships, and deepen those treasured relationships. It's a time to cherish the connections that have been with you through thick and thin and to create new ones that'll bring even more laughter and happiness into your life. Go on—laugh a little louder, love a little deeper, and embrace every chance to connect with the amazing people around you. This is your time to shine, so let your social life sparkle like the champagne you'll be toasting with!

CHAPTER SEVEN

TWO'S COMPANY

Balancing Love, Life, and Personal Space

Retirement lets you turn the page to a brand-new chapter in your love story—one where you and your partner finally have the time to enjoy each other's company without the constant buzz of meetings, deadlines, and never-ending to-do lists. Now, it's just the two of you, ready to embrace all the adventures ahead, free from the daily grind. But let's be honest, as with any great story, this new chapter comes with its own mix of excitement and a few plot twists.

With all this newfound time together, you might start noticing some, let's say, "interesting" changes in your relationship dynamics. Suddenly, you're spending more hours together than ever—sharing meals and hobbies and perhaps even discovering quirky habits you didn't know existed! (Who knew your partner had such strong opinions about folding laundry?) While this can be a delightful experience, it also requires a bit of adjustment. After all, even the most loving couples need their own space and time apart to keep the magic alive.

Here's the fun part: retirement allows you to *grow closer, deepen your connection,* and *explore new ways* to keep the romance alive.

Think of it as a fresh start—a fantastic opportunity to rediscover what made you fall head over heels in the first place and to create new memories together. Sure, there might be the occasional moment when you need to navigate a bump or two in the road, but that's all part of the journey, right?

Now's the time to embrace this as an excellent opportunity to strengthen your partnership. With a bit of patience, some open communication, and a sprinkle of creativity, you'll find that this chapter of your love story can be one of the most fulfilling, joyful, and love-filled yet. Here's to making the most of this beautiful phase in your relationship—quirks and all!

— The Importance of Communication —

Let's be honest—communication is the secret sauce that keeps any relationship thriving. Now that you're spending more time together in retirement, keeping those lines of communication wide open is more critical than ever. After all, you've got a lot of life left to live together, and talking things through is the best way to ensure smooth sailing.

Open and honest communication
is about more than just chatting
about your day; it's about *sharing your
thoughts, feelings, and concerns*
without fear of judgment.

When you communicate openly, you build trust, foster understanding, and create a safe space where you can freely express yourselves. It's like having a safety net to catch you when life gets a little wobbly.

How do you keep communication flowing smoothly?

Start with active listening. Really tune in to what your partner is saying—without interrupting or planning your response while they're talking. Give them your full attention, make eye contact, and show that you're genuinely interested. Sometimes, just being heard is all it takes to make someone feel valued and loved.

Next up, express your needs clearly. It's easy to assume your partner knows what you're thinking, but let's face it—no one's a mind reader! If something's on your mind, speak up. Whether it's needing a bit more personal space or wanting to try a new activity together, sharing your thoughts directly (but kindly) can prevent misunderstandings and keep you both on the same page.

Speaking of misunderstandings, let me tell you about the time my Uncle Jack and Aunt Betty had a classic communication mix-up.

Aunt Betty thought Uncle Jack wanted to start a garden together, so she went all out and bought every gardening tool imaginable. It turns out that Uncle Jack just wanted to "plant" himself in a lawn chair with a good book. They had a good laugh about it, and it became one of their favorite stories to tell—once they cleared up the confusion, of course!

And remember, communication is a two-way street. It's just as important to be open to your partner's needs and feelings as it is to express your own. Practicing patience, empathy, and a good sense of humor will keep the conversation light, positive, and productive.

Compromise and Flexibility

Ah, compromise—the magical ingredient that keeps relationships running smoothly, especially when you're spending more time together in retirement. Think of it as the art of give and take, where both partners find a happy middle ground.

Compromise isn't about one person winning and the other losing; it's about finding solutions that make both of you feel *heard, valued, and content.*

In any partnership, disagreements are bound to pop up now and then. Maybe you're itching to head out on a spontaneous adventure while your partner would instead enjoy a quiet day at home. Or perhaps you've got different ideas about how to spend your newfound free time. This is where the beauty of compromise comes in. By meeting each other halfway, you can create harmony and avoid those pesky conflicts that can dampen your day.

For example, You're planning your weekend and all set for a nature hike, but your partner prefers to catch up on their favorite TV series. Instead of turning it into a tug-of-war, try finding a solution that works for both of you. How about a shorter hike in the morning, followed by a cozy afternoon binge-watching together? This way, you both get to enjoy what you love, and no one feels left out.

Flexibility goes hand in hand with compromise. It's about being open to new ideas, willing to adjust plans, and sometimes even stepping out of your comfort zone. Maybe your partner wants to try a new hobby, like pottery or ballroom dancing, that doesn't quite excite you. Instead of saying "no" immediately, why not give it a shot? You might surprise yourself and find a new passion—or at least share a few laughs along the way.

Nurturing the Relationship:

Even in retirement, the spark in your relationship deserves to be celebrated, fanned, and kept burning brightly. Nurturing your relationship isn't just about grand gestures; it's the little things, the everyday moments of connection, that truly strengthen your bond and keep the love alive.

Start with the small gestures—they can make a world of difference. A simple compliment, a warm hug, or a surprise cup of coffee in the morning can brighten your partner's day and show them how much they mean to you. These tiny acts of kindness and thoughtfulness are like love notes written in the language of everyday life. They remind your partner they're cherished, even in the most ordinary moments.

Regular check-ins are another way to keep your relationship strong. It's easy to get caught up in the retirement routine, but taking the time to connect with each other is crucial. Set aside a few minutes each day to talk about your thoughts, feelings, and what's on your mind. Whether during a morning walk, over dinner, or just before bed, these heart-to-heart conversations help you stay in tune with each other's needs and keep your relationship on track.

And let's not forget about the romance. Maintaining affection and keeping the romance alive doesn't have to be elaborate or expensive. Sometimes, it's as simple as holding hands during a stroll, sharing a dance in the living room, or planning a special date night. These moments of intimacy and connection are the glue that binds your relationship together, making your partnership a habit and a heartfelt choice you make every day.

Strengthening the Bond
Tips for Balancing Time Together with Personal Space

In retirement, you and your partner are likely spending more time together than ever—an outstanding prospect, but one that calls for a bit of balance. Finding that sweet spot between togetherness and personal space is vital to keeping your relationship joyful.

Just because you're both home *doesn't mean* you must be joined at the hip.

It's perfectly healthy (and beneficial!) to spend some time apart, doing things that rejuvenate you. Maybe one of you enjoys a quiet morning with a book while the other takes a brisk walk. Scheduling individual activities, like solo hobbies or exercise, can be a game-changer. This time apart isn't a weakness; it's a way to recharge so that when you come back together, you're both energized and ready to share the best of yourselves.

Setting Joint Goals
Crafting a Shared Vision for Retirement

With more time on your hands, retirement is the perfect moment to dream big and plan for the future—side by side.

Start by having a laid-back chat about what excites both of you. What's on your bucket list? Are there places you've always wanted to visit or hobbies you've been itching to try? Make it fun—grab a cup of coffee and a notepad, and start brainstorming. Maybe it's cooking classes in Tuscany or growing a garden that would make any neighbor green with envy. As you share your individual desires, you'll start to find common ground, and that's where the magic happens.

Once you've pinpointed some shared dreams, break them down into doable steps. If travel is on the list, decide where to go first and start planning the details. The same goes for hobbies—if photography is calling your name, look for local classes or plan weekend outings to practice your new skills.

Ensuring you are aligned on finances is key, too. Make sure your retirement dreams are both exciting and sustainable. Talk about your budget and how it fits with your goals. The joy of setting joint goals lies in the journey itself—planning together, working together, and ultimately, enjoying the fruits of your labor hand in hand.

Communication Tools

Strengthening Relationships
and Avoiding Misunderstandings

Excellent communication is one of the biggest secrets to a happy relationship, especially in retirement when you spend more time together than ever. With all this newfound togetherness, it's wise to have a few tricks up your sleeve to keep things smooth and avoid those pesky misunderstandings.

First up, let's talk about active listening. Picture yourself on a game show; the grand prize is a deeper connection with your partner. To win, all you have to do is really listen—nod, maybe throw in a "Hmm, that's interesting!" or "I see what you mean."

> ## Active listening isn't just waiting for your turn to talk; it's *genuinely tuning in.*

You'd be amazed at how much smoother things go when both of you feel heard.

Next, there's the magical "I" statement. Instead of saying, "You never do the dishes," try, "I feel really appreciated when you help with the dishes." It's like relationship jiu-jitsu—gentle but effective.

And don't forget your relationship tune-ups! A weekly check-in, maybe during your "Sunday Sit-Down," can do wonders. Chat about anything on your mind, from little annoyances to big dreams. Throw in some tech tools like shared calendars or to-do lists, and you're all set.

THE RETIRED COUPLE'S PLAYBOOK
ACTIVITIES TO STRENGTHEN YOUR BOND

With more time on your hands, it's the perfect moment to dive into activities that keep the spark alive and help you create new memories together. From playful date nights to shared hobbies, this section is packed with ideas to bring joy, laughter, and connection to your relationship. Whether exploring new places, learning something new, or simply enjoying each other's company, these activities are designed to deepen your connection and keep your relationship thriving in this exciting chapter of life.

1. Date Nights with a Twist

Date nights don't have to be the same old dinner-and-a-movie routine—retirement is the perfect time to add some spice and creativity to your evenings together! Maybe transform your living room into a cozy Parisian café with French music, a candlelit dinner, and a decadent dessert. Or why not pack a picnic and head to a nearby park for an evening under the stars? You could even make it a themed affair, like an Italian night with homemade pizza and a classic Italian film.

Surprise outings are another fun way to keep things fresh. Take turns planning a secret adventure for the other, like a visit to a local art gallery, a sunset hike, or a spontaneous road trip to a quaint nearby town. The key is to keep the excitement alive by trying new things and stepping out of your usual routine.

Regular date nights, filled with these little twists, are a wonderful way to *keep the romance alive and deepen your connection.*

Plus, they give you something to look forward to, adding a sense of adventure and spontaneity to your relationship.

2. Nurturing Relationships in Special Ways

Nurturing your relationship in unique ways adds little sprinkles of joy to your everyday life—small acts that show appreciation can make all the difference. Start with a simple but powerful gesture: love notes. Tuck a sweet message into your partner's jacket pocket, leave a sticky note on the bathroom mirror, or send a surprise text just to say, "I'm thinking of you." These little reminders of love can brighten your partner's day and keep the connection strong.

Surprise gestures are another delightful way to show you care. How about planning a spontaneous breakfast in bed with all your partner's favorite treats? Or maybe set up a cozy corner with their favorite book and a warm cup of tea ready for them after a long day? Even something as simple as bringing home their favorite snack from the grocery store can be a sweet surprise that shows you're thinking of them.

Celebrating small milestones together can also strengthen your bond. Whether it's the anniversary of your first date or just making it through a tough week, take a moment to acknowledge and celebrate these moments. Plan a special dinner, toast with a glass of wine, or enjoy a simple walk together to mark the occasion.

3. Finding Shared Hobbies

Finding shared hobbies brings you closer, creates lasting memories, and adds an extra layer of joy to your relationship. Envision the two of you, spending a sunny afternoon in the garden, planting flowers side by side, or hiking a scenic trail where every step is a shared adventure. These moments, filled with laughter and teamwork, help you bond over something you both enjoy.

Gardening, for example, is not just about growing plants; it's about nurturing something together, watching it bloom, and enjoying the fruits (or flowers) of your labor. Hiking offers a similar sense of achievement as you explore new paths and discover beautiful landscapes together, creating memories that will last a lifetime.

Photography is another fantastic hobby that lets you see the world through each other's eyes. Whether you're capturing sunsets, wildlife, or candid moments with each other, photography allows you to share perspectives and appreciate the beauty around you.

These shared hobbies
give you time to connect,
learn from each other,
and *celebrate your successes together*.

They turn ordinary days into extraordinary ones, filled with the kind of joy that only comes from doing something you love with someone you love.

4. Cooking Together

Cooking together as a couple is fun, tasty, and brings you closer in the most delightful way. Think about it - the two of you in the kitchen, chopping, stirring, and laughing as you create a delicious meal from scratch. It's an experience that blends creativity, teamwork, and a sprinkle of romance.

Why not plan themed cooking nights to make cooking together even more exciting? One evening, you could whisk yourselves away to Italy with a homemade pizza and pasta night, complete with some Italian music in the background. Another night, spice things up with a Mexican fiesta, complete with tacos, guacamole, and maybe a margarita or two. You can also take turns choosing the menu, surprising each other with new recipes, or recreating your all-time favorite dishes.

Working side by side in the kitchen strengthens *communication and teamwork.*

You'll find that coordinating who does what and cheering each other on as you perfect a dish helps you bond in a relaxed and enjoyable setting. Plus, there's something incredibly satisfying about sitting down together to enjoy a meal you've created with love. So, grab those aprons, fire up the stove, and let the culinary adventures begin!

5. Traveling Together

Traveling together opens a treasure chest of new experiences, each adventure bringing you closer and creating memories that will sparkle for years. Whether you're off on a spontaneous day trip, planning a cozy weekend getaway, or setting out on a more extended vacation, the joy of exploring new places as a couple is unmatched.

Start by sitting down together and dreaming up your next destination. Maybe you're both drawn to the tranquility of a beachside escape or perhaps the excitement of a bustling city has been calling your names.

The key is finding destinations that *cater to your interests and comfort levels.*

If one of you loves hiking and the other prefers museums, look for a spot that offers a bit of both. This way, you can enjoy the trip together while exploring your individual passions.

As you plan, keep the journey as enjoyable as the destination. Road trips with a well-curated playlist, scenic train rides, or even just packing a picnic for a day at a local park can turn any trip into a special occasion. The shared experience of discovering new places, trying local foods, and navigating new environments will deepen your bond, turning each journey into a cherished chapter in your love story.

So, grab your bags, map out your next adventure, and get ready to explore the world hand in hand. Traveling together is more than just seeing new sights—it's about creating a lifetime of shared memories and growing closer with every step.

6. Attending Classes Together

Attending classes together is like opening a new chapter in your relationship, filled with discovery, laughter, and a whole lot of adventure. Whether you're whipping up gourmet dishes in a cooking class, twirling your way through a dance course, or mastering the art of a new language, learning something new as a duo is a recipe for fun and connection.

How fun would it be to perfect a salsa dance routine with your partner or finally nail that tricky soufflé together? These shared experiences aren't just about acquiring new skills but about building memories, one class at a time. You'll find yourselves laughing at the missteps, celebrating the little victories, and cheering each other on as you both step out of your comfort zones.

The beauty of taking classes together lies in the *teamwork* and *collaboration* it fosters.

You'll be each other's biggest supporters, motivating one another to keep going even when the going gets tough. These shared learning experiences can reignite a spark of curiosity and excitement in your relationship, giving you something new to look forward to and talk about.

So, why not sign up for that pottery class you've always talked about or finally learn how to cook that five-course meal you've dreamed of serving? It's not just about the skills you'll acquire—it's about the joy of discovering them together.

7. Game Nights

Game nights are the perfect way to sprinkle a little extra joy into your relationship. Picture this: the two of you, cozied up on a Friday night, surrounded by snacks, laughter, and a healthy dose of friendly competition. Whether you're strategizing over a game of chess, solving a tricky puzzle, or racing against the clock in a room escape challenge, these nights are about having fun and reconnecting with your playful side.

Board games like Scrabble, Monopoly, or Catan are classics that never fail to bring out the best (and sometimes the most competitive!) in us. They're great for sparking conversations, sharing a few laughs, and even uncovering a hidden competitive streak. If you're in the mood for something a little quicker, card games like Uno or Rummy can be just as entertaining and are perfect for those spontaneous game nights when you just want to relax and enjoy each other's company.

Puzzles are another fantastic way to spend quality time together. Whether it's a 1,000-piece landscape or a brain-bending 3D puzzle, working together to complete the picture can be incredibly satisfying—and gives you plenty of time to chat and bond along the way. And for those nights when you're feeling adventurous, why not try a room escape game? Whether you tackle it in person or with a box set at home, these games require teamwork, quick thinking, and plenty of communication—key ingredients for any successful relationship.

The real magic of game nights is in the *laughter* and *light-heartedness* they bring.

They remind us not to take life too seriously, to enjoy the moment, and to cherish the time spent together. Grab your favorite games, set the mood with some music and snacks, and let the fun begin!

8. Movie Night

Movie nights at home are the perfect excuse to snuggle up, unwind, and enjoy some quality time together. Turn your family room into a cozy retreat, where you can escape into your favorite films or discover something new, all while munching on delicious snacks that match the night's theme. It's the ultimate recipe for a relaxed and joyful evening.

Start by picking a selection of films that you both love or dive into a new release you've been curious about. Feeling adventurous? Why not plan a "movie marathon" with a series you've meant to watch or re-watch? From Harry Potter to The Lord of the Rings, or even a classic trilogy like Back to the Future, there's something magical about diving into a world that unfolds over several hours.

To make the night extra special, get creative with *themed snacks.*

Watching a rom-com? How about heart-shaped cookies or strawberries dipped in chocolate? If you're in the mood for an action-packed thriller, nachos with all the fixings might be just the ticket. And don't forget the popcorn! It's a movie night staple, and you can jazz it up with flavored seasonings or drizzle it with a bit of melted butter.

Set the mood with soft lighting, maybe even some fairy lights or candles, and grab a few cozy blankets and pillows to create a comfortable nest. Then, just press play, relax and enjoy the journey through the silver screen. Movie nights at home are mainly about the memories you create together, one movie at a time.

9. Conversation Starter Questions

Sometimes, it's easy to fall into the same old conversations, even after years of being together. That's where conversation starter questions come in—little sparks to reignite the flame of curiosity and connection between you and your partner. Whether you've been married for decades or are just beginning your retirement journey together, these questions can open up new avenues of understanding, laughter, and discovery.

Imagine sitting down together, perhaps with a glass of wine or a cup of tea, and asking each other something unexpected, like, "If you could relive one day from our time together, what would it be?" or "What's a dream you've never told me about?" These questions can lead to stories you've never shared, dreams you didn't know you had in common, and even those lighthearted, fun moments that bring joy to your day.

To make it even easier, downloadable conversation starter sets are available online, tailored specifically for couples. Print them out, cut them into little cards, and draw one randomly during dinner or before bed. It's a simple way to add a bit of excitement and depth to your everyday chats.

These questions do not just pass the time—they help you learn more about each other, even after all these years. They're an excellent tool for deepening your bond, sparking meaningful discussions, and keeping the lines of communication open, ensuring your relationship continues to grow and flourish.

Here are
20 QUESTIONS
to spark an engaging
conversation.

10. Volunteering Together

Volunteering together will add a whole new layer of love and purpose to your relationship. When you and your partner team up to give back, you make a positive impact on your community, and you strengthen your bond in a meaningful way. Think of how nice it would be - the two of you side by side, planting trees in a local park, serving meals at a shelter, or helping out at a community event— each act of kindness bringing you closer together while making the world a little brighter.

One of the most significant benefits of volunteering as a couple is the shared sense of purpose it brings. It's an opportunity to work together toward a common goal, which can be incredibly fulfilling. Plus, volunteering often involves meeting new people, which can expand your social circle and add a bit of adventure to your routine.

So, how do you find the perfect volunteer opportunity?

Start by chatting about what causes or activities resonate with both of you. Do you both love animals? Consider volunteering at a local animal shelter. Are you passionate about the environment? Look into community clean-up projects or tree-planting events. If helping people in need is close to your heart, food banks and homeless shelters are always looking for extra hands.

Once you've narrowed down your interests, check out local community centers, churches, or online platforms like VolunteerMatch to find opportunities that align with your passions. Don't be afraid to try out a few different activities until you find the one that really clicks for both of you. The key is to enjoy the experience and to cherish the time you spend together making a difference.

In the end, volunteering as a couple isn't just about giving back—it's about growing together, discovering new strengths in each other, and finding joy in the shared journey of making the world a better place.

GROWING TOGETHER WITH LOVE AND LAUGHTER

Retirement gives you both the chance to rekindle that old spark while navigating the occasional quirks of togetherness. Imagine it as your favorite sitcom, where the plot twist is that you and your partner are suddenly co-stars in each other's daily lives. Some days, it's a romantic comedy; other days, maybe a little more like a reality show!

As you cozy up to this new phase of your lives, finding the right balance between snuggling up and giving each other breathing room is crucial. Picture it like dancing a tango—sometimes you come together in a passionate embrace, and sometimes you step back to give each other the space to twirl solo.

It's all about *hitting that sweet spot* where you enjoy shared moments and respect each other's need for a little "me time."

Retirement is your backstage ticket to reconnect with why you fell in love in the first place—whether through shared goals, tackling new adventures, or simply laughing at the silly stuff. (Because, let's be honest, the little quirks that once seemed endearing might now require a bit more patience!) The more you communicate, compromise, and throw in a dash of creativity, the more you'll find yourselves writing the best scenes of your life together.

Why not dive head-first into this new chapter with a playful spirit? After all, your retirement years are your time to shine, to rediscover love in all its forms, and to turn even the simplest of moments into memories that'll keep you laughing for years to come. Grab that pen—or maybe a margarita—and start crafting your next great adventure together. The best is yet to come!

CHAPTER EIGHT

MONEY MATTERS

Surviving Without a Paycheck

The paycheck may have waved goodbye, but the good times are here to stay! Now, before splurging on that dream vacation to the moon, let's talk about the key to living your best-retired life: financial planning.

You see, just because the regular income stream has taken a break *doesn't mean the fun has to stop.*

Oh no, with some smart planning, your money can stretch further than a grandkid's birthday balloon. And guess what? You can still enjoy those little luxuries—like treating yourself to that extra scoop of ice cream—without sweating the small stuff.

Balancing frugality with fun is almost better than mastering the perfect dance routine. Sure, you'll need to shuffle around some numbers, but there's always room for a twirl of joy here and there. So, buckle up, my friend! With a pinch of planning and a dash of budgeting magic, you'll be well on your way to a retirement that's not just financially sound but also brimming with laughter, leisure, and a whole lot of life.

Why Planning Is Your Financial Superpower

Budgeting might not sound like the most thrilling part of retirement, but trust me, it's your financial superpower. Budgeting is your secret weapon, ensuring you're ready for anything life throws your way—from that unexpected plumbing bill to a spontaneous weekend getaway.

Now, before you start worrying that budgeting means turning into a penny-pincher, let's set the record straight. Budgeting isn't about denying yourself life's little pleasures. It's about making sure those pleasures are possible without causing you any stress. It's having your cake, eating it, and knowing there's still enough left over for dessert tomorrow.

Start by taking a good look at where your money's going. Regularly checking in on your spending helps you spot areas where you might need to tighten the reins and others where you can afford a little extra flourish. Maybe you've got a soft spot for fancy coffees or a weakness for online shopping. You can still indulge with a bit more finesse with a budget.

The beauty of budgeting is that it *gives you control.*

You decide what's worth spending on and what can take a backseat. Want to splurge on a cruise? Great! Just tweak your budget, adjust a few expenses, and off you go, sailing into the sunset with peace of mind and a cocktail in hand.

You mustn't think of budgeting as a restriction. See it as your super-power—guiding you through retirement confidently, allowing you to enjoy the things you love without worrying about the bottom line.

Practical Tips and Strategies

Rainy Day Ready: Creating a Financial Emergency Plan.

Let's face it—life has a knack for throwing curveballs. Sometimes, it's a leaky roof; other times, that surprise dental bill leaves you wincing. But with a solid financial emergency plan, those unexpected expenses won't have you scrambling for loose change under the couch cushions.

First things first, start by setting aside a „rainy day fund." This is your financial umbrella, ready to pop open when life's little storms hit. Aim to build up three to six months' worth of living expenses in a separate savings account. This might sound like a lot, but consider it your financial security blanket—there when you need it, comforting even when you don't.

Now, don't worry if you're not there yet. Start small. Maybe skip that extra fancy latte this week and toss the savings into your emergency fund instead. Every little bit adds up, and before you know it, you'll have a nice cushion to soften the blow of any unexpected costs.

Another tip? Review your insurance policies. Make sure you're covered for those big-ticket surprises—home repairs, medical emergencies, and the like. You don't want to discover you're underinsured when the roof decides to spring a leak.

Being rainy day ready isn't about living in fear of what could go wrong. It's about planning for peace of mind, knowing that whatever life throws your way, you're financially prepared to handle it with a smile. Plus, with your emergency fund in place, you can rest easy, knowing you've got a safety net that's as solid as they come.

Taking Advantage of Discounts and Deals:

Who doesn't love a good bargain? Especially when you can claim the title of Savvy Senior Shopper. The world of discounts and deals is your oyster, and plenty of pearls are waiting to be discovered.

First, let's talk about those magical words: „senior discount." These two little words can turn a regular day into a shopping spree with a side of savings. From restaurants to retail stores, many places offer discounts for seniors—you just need to know where to look. So, don't be shy—ask about senior discounts wherever you go. That coffee shop you love might shave a few cents off your daily brew, and the local movie theater could have a special rate that makes date night even sweeter.

If you want to expand your discount horizons, AARP is your golden ticket. Membership unlocks a treasure chest of savings on travel, dining, insurance, and more. You'll feel like a VIP with access to deals that keep your wallet happy while you enjoy life's little luxuries.

Don't forget about senior discount days—many grocery stores and department stores designate a day of the week when seniors can save even more. Mark it on your calendar, make a list, and head out knowing you're getting the best bang for your buck.

And for the tech-savvy, online deals are your new best friend. Websites like Groupon and RetailMeNot are bursting with discounts on everything from dinner to digital gadgets. Sign up for their newsletters and let the deals come to you.

Being a savvy senior isn't just about pinching pennies—it's about stretching those dollars to enjoy life to the fullest, with plenty of change left over for the next adventure.

Monthly Money Tune-Up: Reviewing Your Budget.

Let's talk about the monthly money tune-up—your financial check-in that keeps everything running smoothly, like oiling the gears of a well-loved bicycle. Now, before you roll your eyes at the idea of „budgeting," let's agree to spice things up a bit. After all, what's more satisfying than seeing your money working for you, with a little left over for that impromptu ice cream run?

Start by setting aside some time each month to give your budget a good once-over. Grab a cup of coffee, sit down with your favorite pen (or budgeting app if you're fancy), and look at where your money went last month. Did those grocery bills sneak up on you? Did you splurge a bit too much on new garden gnomes? This is your chance to see what's working and what needs a tweak.

The goal here isn't to stress over every penny but to ensure your spending aligns with your goals. Maybe that means adjusting your „fun money" allowance if you're planning a big trip or finding a new grocery store with better deals. It's all about making small changes that keep your finances in tip-top shape without feeling like you're sacrificing the good stuff.

And here's the kicker—treat yourself after each budget review. Whether it's a walk in the park, a new book, or, yes, another scoop of that ice cream, reward yourself for staying on track. Who knew budgeting could be this delightful? Keep it light, keep it fun, and watch your financial peace of mind grow month by month.

ACTIVITIES: MAKING MONEY MANAGEMENT FUN

Whoever said managing money had to be a snooze-fest clearly never tried turning it into a game. Think of your finances as a puzzle—each piece you put together brings you closer to the big picture of financial freedom. In this section, we're diving into activities that make money management both bearable and downright enjoyable. From quirky savings plans to hunting down the best deals, these fun and engaging tasks will have you feeling like a financial whiz in no time.

1. Financial Check-Up
Know Where You Stand

It's time for your financial check-up! Don't worry, there are no needles involved—just a good ol' look at where your money's at. Start by taking a deep dive into your assets (what you own), liabilities (what you owe), income (what's coming in), and expenses (where it's all going).

This isn't just a spreadsheet exercise —it's your roadmap to *financial peace of mind.*

I once heard about a retired couple who decided to do a financial check-up after years of coasting along without much thought. They sat down with their coffee, opened their laptop, and started listing everything. Halfway through, the husband suddenly realized they'd been paying for a gym membership they hadn't used in three years. Turns out, their treadmill at home was the only workout they'd been doing—by walking past it every day! They canceled that membership faster than you can say, „financial freedom." They redirected those funds to something they actually enjoyed: a weekly date night.

Use tools like spreadsheets or financial apps to organize your information to make this process smoother. Apps like Mint or YNAB (You Need a Budget) can help you see the big picture at a glance. Once you've got everything laid out, you'll be able to spot where you can make tweaks and adjustments. Who knows? You might even uncover a hidden gym membership or two.

2. Get Your Ducks in a Row
Organize Your Finances

Alright, it's time to get those financial ducks in a row, and no, this doesn't involve actual ducks, but if you want to get some, who's stopping you? Organizing your finances is like tidying up your closet—only instead of discovering that shirt you forgot you had, you might find some cash hiding in forgotten accounts or unnecessary subscriptions.

Ready to declutter your financial life?
Let's get started.

First, you need a system to track your income, expenses, and goals. Think of this as the GPS for your money. Apps like Mint, YNAB, or even a good old-fashioned spreadsheet are great tools for this. Start by listing all your income sources—pensions, savings, and side gigs (even the Etsy shop selling crochet cat hats counts). Next, detail your expenses. Break them into housing, utilities, food, and fun money. Make sure you're as detailed as a detective on a hot case. The more you know, the easier it is to see where you might be able to trim the fat (like streaming services you forgot about).

Now, onto organizing those important documents. This is like creating the ultimate filing system, one that would make Marie Kondo proud. Gather all your financial paperwork—bank statements, insurance policies, investment records—and sort them into folders. You can go old-school with physical files or digital with cloud storage. The key is to create a system that's easy to access and update.

Finally, create a financial calendar. Write down key dates like bill due dates, insurance renewals, and when to check your budget. This way, nothing sneaks up on you. A wall calendar works fine, but if you're more tech-savvy, set up reminders on your phone or a digital calendar like Google Calendar.

Here's a fun tip: Make this process enjoyable by setting small rewards for yourself. After you get everything organized and in order, treat yourself to something fun—maybe that new book you've been eyeing or a walk in the park. By keeping it light and rewarding, you'll find that getting your financial ducks in a row isn't just necessary—it can be downright satisfying.

3. Savings with a Smile
Create a Fun Savings Plan

Who says saving money has to be a dull, joy-sucking task? Let's turn that piggy bank into a party pig with a savings plan that's as fun as it is effective. First up, let's talk numbers—because nothing says „fun" like setting some good, old-fashioned financial goals.

Start by figuring out how much you need to save each month. This doesn't have to be rocket science. Break it down into two buckets: one for your big dreams (like that trip to Tuscany) and one for life's little surprises (like when your washing machine decides it's retiring, too). Look at your income and expenses, then decide on a realistic amount you can comfortably tuck away each month.

Now, here's where the fun kicks in—tracking your progress! Create a savings chart that turns your goals into something you can see and celebrate. You can draw a giant thermometer on a poster board and color it in as your savings grow. Alternatively, use an app like Qapital to set visual goals and even round up your purchases to add to your savings. If you're a tech fan, check out apps like Digit, which sneakily saves small amounts without you even noticing.

Want to keep things interesting?
Set *mini-milestones* along the way.

Each time you reach a certain amount, reward yourself with something small and enjoyable—like a fancy coffee or a night out. These little celebrations make saving feel less like a chore and more like a game. And hey, who doesn't love a game where the prize is financial peace of mind?

4. Invest in Your Future
Tips and Tricks for Growing Wealth

Ready to let your money stretch its legs and do some serious heavy lifting? It's time to get those dollars working harder than ever so you can kick back and savor the sweet rewards. Let's dive headfirst into the world of investments—because who doesn't love the idea of money multiplying like rabbits?

First, let's talk about the investment basics: stocks, bonds, and retirement accounts. Stocks are like that unpredictable cousin at family gatherings. Sometimes, they surprise you with something amazing; other times, they keep you on your toes. On the other hand, bonds are like that dependable friend who's always there for you—steady, reliable, and with a bit less risk. Then we have retirement accounts, like IRAs and 401(k)s, which are your financial besties, quietly working behind the scenes to make sure your golden years are, well, golden.

But here's where it gets really exciting—let's talk dividends. They're regular payments made by companies to shareholders, a little thank you for holding onto their stock. Essentially, you get paid just for owning shares! Companies that pay dividends are often well-established and financially stable, so they can be a great way to generate passive income. If the idea of getting regular checks in the mail (or, more likely, direct deposits) sounds appealing, look into dividend-paying stocks. For more detailed information, check out resources like The Little Book of Big Dividends by Charles B. Carlson. It's packed with insights on how to build a dividend-focused portfolio.

If you're wondering where to begin
your investment journey,
don't fret—there's *plenty of guidance*
out there.

Start with The Intelligent Investor by Benjamin Graham. It's the investment bible, offering timeless wisdom on how to grow your wealth while managing risk. For something a bit more modern and accessible, try A Random Walk Down Wall Street by Burton G. Malkiel. It's like the must-see series of investment books—educational, engaging, and perfect for anyone wanting to get savvy with their savings.

And let's not forget we're living in the digital age! Take advantage of online resources like Investopedia for the down-and-dirty details or apps like Robinhood if you're ready to start trading with zero commissions. Remember, the key to successful investing is starting early, staying consistent, and learning. Happy investing!

5. Budgeting Fun
The Happy Planner Approach

Whoever said budgeting had to be boring clearly never got their hands on a set of colorful pens and a happy planner! Here's the secret: creating a budget can be as enjoyable as planning a vacation.

It's your roadmap
to your *financial freedom*,
with a few fun pit stops
along the way.

Start by dividing your budget into three main categories: essentials, savings, and fun money. Essentials are the must-haves: rent, groceries, and keeping the lights on. Savings are your safety net, building a cushion for those „just in case" moments. And fun money? That's your well-deserved treat for all the hard work. Whether it's a night out, a new gadget, or that cooking class you've been eyeing, fun money keeps life exciting without breaking the bank.

Now, here's where the real fun begins. Grab some color-coded pens or highlighters and assign a color to each category. Your budget suddenly looks less like a daunting spreadsheet and more like a piece of art. If you're tech-savvy, try budget apps like You Need A Budget (YNAB) or EveryDollar. They're like personal finance coaches that fit right in your pocket, reminding you to stick to your plan while making it easy to track every penny.

Speaking of tracking, let me tell you about my friend, Betty. She decided to tackle her budget with the same enthusiasm she brings to her weekly bingo night. Betty went all out—bought a happy planner, labeled everything, and even threw in some motivational stickers. She had one sticker that said, „Don't spend it all in one place unless it's on ice cream!" Every month, Betty would sit down with a cup of tea and her planner, delighted to see how much she had saved for her next big adventure—visiting all the ice cream shops in her town! Betty's planner didn't just keep her finances on track; it made her look forward to budgeting as much as she did her ice cream splurges.

Why not add a bit of joy to your budgeting routine? By making it colorful, creative, and, yes—even fun—you'll find that managing your money feels less like a chore and more like a celebration of all the fantastic things you can achieve. Happy planning, and don't forget to add a little sprinkle of fun to your financial journey!

Download your
budget plan template
HERE!

6. Financial Confessions
Let's Talk Money, Honey!

Money talk has long been considered taboo, tucked away like that mysterious tin of Christmas cookies in the back of your cupboard. But here's the thing: bringing those financial worries and goals out into the open can do wonders for your peace of mind and bank account. Imagine the relief of sharing tips and tricks with friends and realizing that you're not alone in navigating the maze of retirement finances.

Talking openly about money
can help you *uncover new strategies,*
gain fresh perspectives, and even
turn those budget blues into *budget bliss*!

One way to get the conversation rolling is to start a monthly budget club. Picture this: you and a group of friends, cozying up with a cup of coffee (or something stronger!) and chatting about your financial wins and woes. Share the deals you scored, the challenges you faced, and the goals you're working toward. Not only will you learn from each other, but you'll also be able to cheer each other on and keep those financial goals front and center.

And here's a fun twist—have I mentioned my friend, Jeannette? She started a budget club, which quickly became her month's highlight. They once had a „Who Found the Weirdest Discount" contest. Jeannette won with a hilarious story about getting half off a cemetery plot „for future use"—talk about long-term planning!

By turning financial discussions into a regular, open, and light-hearted part of your routine, you'll find that those money matters aren't nearly as scary as they once seemed. So, grab your friends, brew some coffee, and let's talk money, honey!

7. Frugal but Fabulous
Hobbies on a Budget

Who says hobbies have to cost an arm and a leg? You can explore new passions with a bit of creativity without draining your retirement fund.

> **Here's how to keep your hobbies fabulous and frugal!**

Gardening

Gardening is a fantastic way to grow both your veggies and your sense of accomplishment. Start small with a few pots of herbs or tomatoes on your balcony, and you'll soon be harvesting more than just savings. Seeds are cheap, and watching your garden flourish is a joy that keeps on giving—plus, fresh basil on your pasta? Pure bliss. And if you're lucky, your green thumb might even lead to a side hustle at the local farmer's market. (Just don't tell your neighbors, or they'll ask for free tomatoes all summer!)

Crafting

Crafting is another budget-friendly way to get those creative juices flowing. Whether you're knitting scarves, making homemade candles, or upcycling old furniture, the possibilities are endless—and so are the savings. Hit up thrift stores for supplies or raid your own closet for materials. Online platforms like Pinterest and YouTube are brimming with tutorials that can turn you into a crafting

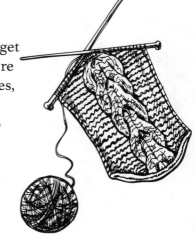

maestro without spending a fortune. You might even create gifts that are so fabulous that your friends will wonder how you can afford them!

Cooking

Cooking is a delicious hobby that can save you big bucks. Experimenting with new recipes is like a mini culinary adventure every time you step into the kitchen. Take advantage of free online cooking classes on platforms like Coursera or YouTube, where celebrity chefs spill their secrets. Before you know it, you'll be whipping up gourmet meals that rival your favorite restaurants—for a fraction of the cost. Bonus: Leftovers mean you're practically printing money.

Community Classes

And don't forget about community classes. Many local centers offer free or low-cost workshops on everything from photography to pottery. It's a great way to learn new skills, meet new people, and enjoy your retirement without burning through your savings.

Get your gardening gloves, knitting needles, or spatula, and take a leap right into your next hobby. Your wallet—and your sense of fulfillment—will thank you!

8. Deal Detective
Hunting for Bargains and Steals

Ready to unleash your inner Sherlock Holmes on the world of discounts? With a little sleuthing, you can snag the best deals on everyday items without breaking a sweat—or the bank.

Let's dive into the art of *bargain hunting*!

Firstly, get your smartphone ready because apps are your new best friend. Download apps like Honey and Rakuten to automatically find coupon codes and cash-back offers when you shop online. No need to scour the Internet for those elusive promo codes—these apps do the heavy lifting for you, leaving you with more time (and money) to enjoy retirement. There's also Flipp, an app that lets you browse weekly ads from your favorite stores and even compiles coupons that can be used in-store. Now, that's smart shopping!

Regarding online resources, websites like Slickdeals and CamelCamelCamel are absolute goldmines. Slickdeals lets you tap into a community of deal hunters who share the best finds across the web. At the same time, CamelCamelCamel tracks price histories on Amazon so you can strike when the price is right. Talk about leveling up your shopping game!

Don't overlook the good old-fashioned local sales, either. Keep an eye out for clearance racks, especially during end-of-season sales when stores practically give things away. If you're really dedicated, you can even ask the store manager about upcoming sales or discounts. You'd be surprised how much you can save just by asking a simple question!

And here's a pro tip: timing is everything. Shop for holiday decorations right after the holiday, snag winter coats in spring and buy electronics during major sales events like Black Friday. This timing strategy can save you big bucks, and who doesn't love getting something great at a fraction of the price?

So, put on that detective hat and start hunting for those bargains. With these tools and strategies, you'll be the Sherlock of savings, uncovering deals that make every shopping trip feel like a win!

9. Zero-Dollar Entertainment
Fun That Doesn't Cost a Dime

Who says you need a wallet full of cash to have a good time? There's a whole world of fun out there that won't cost you a penny—and it's yours for the taking!

Let's look into some fantastic *zero-dollar entertainment ideas* that will keep you smiling and your budget intact.

Start with the great outdoors. Hiking is a surefire way to enjoy nature, exercise, and soak up some sunshine, all for a low, low free price! Check out local trails in your area using apps like AllTrails and set off on an adventure. You'll discover scenic views, hidden gems, and maybe even a few new friends along the way. Plus, there's nothing like that post-hike glow—nature's very own spa treatment!

If you're looking to give back while having fun, consider volunteering. From animal shelters to community gardens, there's no shortage of places that could use an extra pair of hands. Volunteering isn't just good for the soul; it's also an excellent way to meet people, learn new skills, and feel connected to your community. And who knows? You might just find your new favorite hobby while you're at it.

Now, let's talk about the magic of your local library. Libraries aren't just for borrowing books (though that's always a delight); they're also a hub of free events and activities. Think movie nights, book clubs, crafting sessions, and even tech workshops. Pop by your library and grab a calendar of events—it's like a treasure map leading to endless free fun!

And don't forget about good old-fashioned game nights at home. Pull out those dusty board games, fire up a trivia app, or even host a themed charades night. The laughter and friendly competition are priceless, and the best part? No need to spend a dime.

So go ahead and embrace the zero-dollar lifestyle! These activities prove that you don't need to spend big to have big fun. It's all about creativity, community, and enjoying the simple pleasures in life—no wallet required!

10. Thrifty Travels
Budget-Friendly Adventures

Who says you need a royal fortune to explore the world? With a bit of savvy planning and a pinch of creativity, you can enjoy amazing adventures without emptying your wallet. First off, let's talk about timing. Off-season trips are your golden ticket to significant savings. It's the same as getting the VIP experience without the VIP price tag—fewer crowds, cheaper flights, and discounted accommodations. For example, a springtime jaunt to Europe can be just as magical as a summer one, minus the inflated costs and selfie-stick traffic jams.

Next, become best friends with discount travel sites. Websites like Skyscanner, Kayak, and Google Flights are perfect for sniffing out the best deals on airfare. And if you're flexible with dates, you can score even more significant savings. Don't forget to check out budget airlines and set up fare alerts to grab those elusive deals when they pop up.

Accommodation-wise, consider alternative options like Airbnb, hostels, or even house swapping if you're feeling adventurous. And for the super thrifty, don't overlook last-minute deals on sites like Hotwire or Priceline.

One of my favorite tips: embrace the joy of slow travel. By spending more time in one place, you can really soak in the local culture, find hidden gems, and save on transportation costs. Plus, you'll have plenty of stories to tell—like when my coworker, Bill, spent a week in a tiny Italian village, learned to make pasta from a local nonna, and paid less for his entire trip than he would've spent on a weekend in Paris!

What on earth are you waiting for, then?
Pack those bags, and *let your
budget-friendly adventure begin*
—your passport and wallet
will both thank you!

11. Think Outside the Box
Creative Ways to Boost Your Finances

When it comes to managing your finances, sometimes you've got to get a little creative. There are plenty of ways to bring in some extra income beyond traditional routes. One option is to consider starting a side hustle. Whether it's something you're passionate about, like crafting or freelance writing, or a skill you can monetize, like tutoring or consulting, a side hustle can boost your bank account while keeping you busy and engaged.

Another great way to pad your wallet is by selling items you no longer need. We all have things around the house that are gathering dust—old collectibles, unused gadgets, or even furniture sitting in the garage. You can turn those forgotten treasures into cash by having a garage sale or listing them online on platforms like Facebook Marketplace, eBay, or Craigslist. It's a win-win: you declutter your space and earn some extra money in the process.

Don't overlook the value of things you might think are worthless. That old vinyl collection, vintage toys, or even certain types of kitchenware can be worth more than you'd expect. A quick search online can help you determine the value of your items and guide you on where to sell them for the best price.

Thinking outside the box when it comes to your finances doesn't just help you earn extra cash —it's also a fun and rewarding way to *make the most of your resources.*

So, start digging through those closets, see what you can sell, and explore new ways to grow your income. You might be surprised at what you can achieve!

FINANCIAL FREEDOM WITH A SMILE

Let's face it—finding the sweet spot between saving those pennies and enjoying your golden years is like mastering the art of balancing on a tightrope...with a margarita in hand. But here's the good news: with a little financial planning and some creativity, you can savor all the fun that retirement offers without breaking the bank.

Your budget is the ultimate wingman, keeping you steady while you live it up. Keeping an eye on your finances is essential, but treating yourself along the way is equally important. After all, retirement is your time to shine, and who said frugality can't be fabulous?

Plan that trip, pick up that new hobby, and *indulge in the occasional splurge.*

Just remember to keep your financial ducks in a row so that you can enjoy these moments with peace of mind. By balancing frugality with a little bit of flair, you're thriving in retirement, instead of just surviving.

And here's the best part: the more you embrace this balance, the more you'll discover that financial freedom isn't about how much you have but how wisely you use it. It's about living joyfully, laughing often, and making the most of every day. So keep smiling, keep saving, and keep celebrating—your best years are ahead. They're looking bright, fun, and fabulously frugal!

CHAPTER NINE

GRAND ADVENTURE

Travel and Exploration

Retirement: the grand finale where the curtain rises on the rest of your life, and the world becomes your stage! This is your moment to swap the office chair for a window seat on a plane, train, or even a cozy bench in a faraway park.

Travel isn't just for the young and restless—it's for the *wise and wonderful*, too.

And guess what? There's no clock to punch, no deadlines to meet, and definitely no bosses to answer to (except maybe your travel partner, and we know how that goes!).

Travel in retirement isn't just about ticking off bucket-list destinations—it's about filling your days with new sights, sounds, and flavors that keep your spirit lively and your mind sharp. It's about meeting new people, soaking in different cultures, and embracing the joy of the unexpected. Whether you're venturing to far-flung lands or exploring the hidden gems in your own backyard, each journey adds a whole lot of adventure and joy to your retirement.

The Benefits of Travel and Exploration in Retirement

Travel is all about embracing a lifestyle that enriches both body and soul. Every journey, whether near or far, brings with it a world of benefits that go beyond just seeing new sights. From boosting your mental well-being to keeping you physically active and socially connected, the adventures you embark on can turn your golden years into a vibrant, joy-filled chapter of life.

Mental Wellness:

Packing your bags and heading off to new destinations doesn't just lighten your luggage; it lightens your mood, too. Strolling through a bustling market, wandering through ancient ruins, or simply sipping coffee at a quaint café in a foreign land can work wonders for your mental health. There's something about breaking away from the every day that melts stress like butter on a warm croissant in Paris, leaving you happier, more relaxed, and with a spring in your step.

But that's not all. Travel keeps your brain buzzing. Encountering new cultures, languages, and traditions stretches your mental muscles, keeping them toned and agile. It's like a mental workout but way more fun than Sudoku. Plus, seeing the world from different perspectives opens your mind and fills it with fresh ideas, helping you stay sharp and curious. So, the next time someone asks why you're always planning your next getaway, just tell them it's for your mental fitness. Who knew relaxation could be so good for the brain?

Social Connections & Personal Growth:

When you're on the road, making friends becomes as easy as striking up a conversation with the person next to you at a scenic overlook or bonding over a shared confusion about local customs. These encounters often turn into lasting friendships, giving you stories to share and friends to visit across the globe. Who knew your social circle could expand faster than your photo collection?

But let's talk about the perks of stepping out of your comfort zone. Travel is the ultimate test of adaptability, whether navigating a foreign city or trying to figure out how to order dinner in a language you don't speak. Each little challenge you face on the road leads to a bit of personal growth. Before you know it, you're no longer just a retiree—you're a seasoned explorer, ready to tackle anything from dodgy street food to the complexities of a foreign transit system. The sense of accomplishment you get from these experiences is like finding that perfect souvenir: priceless, memorable, and uniquely yours.

Physical Benefits of Exploration:

Who needs a gym membership when the whole world is your playground? Traveling is the perfect excuse to keep your body moving in the most enjoyable way. From strolling through bustling markets to hiking up scenic trails, every step you take on your adventures adds more vitality to your life. Your Fitbit will be so impressed that it might throw you a party.

Let's talk about the bonus perks. When you're exploring new places, you naturally find yourself more active—whether you're wandering through ancient ruins, swimming in crystal-clear waters, or just walking around discovering hidden gems in a new city. Plus, travel often nudges you toward healthier eating habits. Fresh, local produce, exotic fruits, and new culinary experiences are a delicious step up from your usual snacks. Before you know it, you're collecting not just souvenirs but health benefits, too. Traveling keeps your body in tip-top shape and makes you feel as vibrant as the places you visit.

Travel as a Source of Joy and Relaxation:

Let's be honest: nothing beats the thrill of ditching your daily routine for a fresh adventure. That endless to-do list at home? Poof—gone, replaced by the blissful freedom of travel. Swapping out grocery runs to explore quaint streets or trading in laundry day for lounging on a sun-soaked beach is the ultimate recipe for joy and relaxation. It's like hitting the reset button on life, with each new destination offering a chance to recharge your batteries in the most amazing way.

And let's talk about the memories—those little nuggets of happiness that stick with you long after you've unpacked your suitcase. Whether laughing over a language mix-up in a bustling market or watching the sunset with your toes in the sand, these moments become the stories you'll cherish and share for years. Travel doesn't just fill your photo albums; it fills your heart with a rich assortment of experiences, each one more colorful and joyful than the last.

Practical Tips and Strategies

When planning your next great adventure, the goal is to keep it stress-free, wallet-friendly, and as smooth as a perfectly packed suitcase. The good news? You don't need to be a seasoned globetrotter to make it happen. With a few handy strategies and the right tools in your travel arsenal, you can navigate the world like a pro, all while staying healthy, safe, and on budget. Ready to explore some practical tips that will have you jet-setting with ease and enjoying every minute of your journey? Let's get to it!

Easy Travel Planning: Stress-Free Strategies.

Planning a trip should be as fun as the adventure itself, without the headaches of missed connections or forgotten essentials. Thanks to some handy travel apps and websites, organizing your journey can be as breezy as a seaside stroll. One suggestion is to try TripIt. It's like having a personal assistant who organizes your travel plans without asking for a raise. It compiles all your bookings—flights, hotels, car rentals—into a single itinerary that's easy to access on your phone. No more digging through emails at the airport gate!

Then there's Kayak, the Sherlock Holmes of travel deals. It sniffs out the best prices on flights, accommodations, and car rentals. The best part? Kayak's price alerts ensure you never miss out on a bargain, so you can save those extra bucks for something more fun, like a souvenir sombrero or a spontaneous dinner at a rooftop restaurant.

When it comes to organizing your trip, start by making a simple itinerary—yes, even if you're more of a free spirit. Include your flight details, accommodation addresses, and key activities you don't want to miss. And hey, remember to leave some room for spontaneity! Because the best adventures often come from wandering off the beaten path, right?

Speaking of beaten paths, there was this one time I decided to wing it on a trip without any planning (rookie mistake, I know). I ended up at a „beachfront" hotel...that was a 30-minute hike from the actual beach. Lesson learned: a little planning goes a long way in ensuring your trip is more paradise and less „Where on earth am I?"

With some prep and the right apps, you'll be sipping piña coladas on the beach instead of frantically searching for your hotel address.

Health and Safety Precautions: Travel with Peace of Mind.

Traveling is all about enjoying the journey, and a little preparation can keep those unexpected bumps in the road from turning into full-blown detours. First things first: packing. Creating a solid checklist can make all the difference between a relaxing vacation and a frantic pharmacy run in a foreign land. Start with the must-haves: medications (don't forget those pesky refills), a compact first-aid kit (because paper cuts from travel brochures are real), and, of course, travel insurance. Yes, it might seem tedious, but trust me, it's your golden ticket to peace of mind when life throws a curveball—like the time when my suitcase decided to take its own vacation to Timbuktu.

Speaking of curveballs, let's not forget the great pandemic of recent history. COVID-19 reminded us all of the importance of staying vigilant about health while traveling. Keep that hand sanitizer handy and maybe pack a few masks—you know, just in case you find yourself in a crowded market or next to a particularly sneezy fellow traveler.

Now, let's talk about keeping your body in tip-top shape on the go. Staying hydrated isn't just for camels—it's your secret weapon against jet lag and travel fatigue. And while it's tempting to dive headfirst into every buffet you encounter, try to balance the indulgence with some lighter, healthier meals. Your stomach (and waistband) will thank you later.

Oh, and one more thing: take breaks! Travel can be exhausting, even when you're having a blast. Give yourself time to recharge, whether it's a quick nap or a leisurely stroll in the park. After all, you're on vacation—you've earned the right to relax!

Managing Travel Budget: Adventure Without Breaking the Bank.

Traveling on a budget doesn't mean skipping all the fun—it's about being smart with your money so you can stretch those dollars into even more adventures. So, let's talk about setting a realistic travel budget. Start by figuring out how much you can comfortably spend without feeling like you'll need to sell your house when you return. Divide your budget into categories: transportation, accommodations, food, and, of course, the all-important „fun money" for those spur-of-the-moment gelato breaks.

Now, for saving tips that are easier than finding the best gelato in Rome. Start putting aside a small amount each month in a dedicated travel fund—because nothing says „vacation" like guilt-free spending. Also, keep an eye out for those sneaky little costs that add up, like baggage fees and airport snacks. Planning ahead can save you from the dreaded „Wait, how much did I spend?" moment when you get home.

Maximizing value is where the real travel magic happens. Look for deals on flights by using fare comparison websites like Kayak or Google Flights, and set up alerts so you can pounce when prices drop. When it comes to accommodations, consider alternatives such as vacation rentals or charming little bed-and-breakfasts—they often give you more bang for your buck than big-name hotels. And don't be shy about hunting for discounts on activities—many cities offer tourist passes that bundle attractions together at a discount, which means more fun for less cash.

Cheap Thrills: Affordable Ways to See the World.

Who says you need to be rolling in dough to roll around the globe? Travel on a budget can be just as thrilling, if not more so, with the right tricks up your sleeve. Let's take a look into some low-cost travel ideas that'll have you jet-setting without emptying your piggy bank.

You might consider house swapping. It's like the ultimate sleepover for adults—except instead of crashing on your friend's couch, you're living it up in their entire house while they're chilling in yours. Websites like HomeExchange make finding a swap that suits your style effortless. If you prefer your home to have wheels, RV trips are a fantastic way to see the world at your own pace. You get to explore, stop wherever you want, and sleep under the stars—all without a hotel bill in sight.

Then there's the magic of off-season travel. Think Paris without the crowds or a tropical beach that's all yours. Off-season trips are not only cheaper but also offer a more relaxed experience. Plus, there's something oddly satisfying about getting a steal on a trip that others pay top dollar for just a few months later.

Now, let's talk discounts. Being a senior has its perks, and travel discounts are some of the best. Many airlines, hotels, and attractions offer special rates for seniors. Group travel deals are another fantastic way to save—round up your friends or join a group tour, and you might find yourself saving a bundle. Budget-friendly accommodations like hostels, guesthouses, or Airbnb can stretch your travel dollars, leaving you more cash for adventure.

ACTIVITIES:
MAKING TRAVEL AND EXPLORATION YOUR NEW HOBBY

Are you ready to make travel your new favorite hobby? Whether you're jet-setting across the globe or exploring the hidden gems in your own backyard, this is your chance to turn every day into an adventure. Forget about just checking places off a list—let's look into experiences that fill your soul with joy and your camera with unforgettable memories. From hiking trails that take your breath away (literally) to discovering the quirky corners of your hometown, these activities are all about embracing the wanderlust within you. Grab your map, dust off those hiking boots, and start planning your next great escape!

1. Plan Your Next Great Escape

Alright, traveler extraordinaire, it's time to plan your next big adventure! Start by letting your mind wander to all those places you've always wanted to visit—be it the charming streets of a European city or the hidden trails of a nearby national park.

The world is your oyster; now's the perfect time to *start cracking it open.*

Begin by jotting down your dream destinations, and don't hold back—this is your chance to let your wanderlust run wild!

Once you've got a list, it's time to get down to business. Grab your laptop, tablet, or good old-fashioned paper map and start plotting. Websites like TripAdvisor and Lonely Planet are your best friends for digging into what makes each destination tick. From must-see landmarks to those off-the-beaten-path gems, these resources will help you uncover all the hidden treasures waiting to be explored.

When it comes to booking, there are some seriously savvy tools at your disposal. Kayak and Skyscanner are brilliant for comparing flights. At the same time, Airbnb and Booking.com have got your accommodations covered—whether you're after a quirky boutique hotel or a cozy cottage by the sea. And don't forget to keep an eye out for deals on sites like Groupon or Travelzoo, where you can snag discounts on everything from guided tours to all-inclusive packages.

2. Travel Your Own Backyard
Become a Tourist in Your City

You don't have to cross oceans or continents to have an adventure. Sometimes, the most delightful discoveries are right under your nose. Becoming a tourist in your own city is almost as much fun as finding hidden treasure in your backyard. Who knew your city had so many gems waiting to be explored? Start by digging into local attractions you've always meant to visit but never got around to—yes, that museum down the street you've walked past a hundred times.

Create a local travel bucket list. Start with the biggies: museums, historical landmarks, and parks. But don't stop there! Dig deeper—seek out quirky local shops, hidden cafes, and those murals or sculptures you've always admired from afar. Is there a park nearby? Spend a day wandering its trails, or pack a picnic and soak up the sun. Maybe there's a botanical garden just waiting to be your new favorite escape. You might find yourself saying, „How have I never been here before?"

Spice things up by setting a theme for each adventure: „Cultural Wednesday" could be for museum hopping, while „Foodie Friday" might see you sampling treats from different bakeries or food trucks around town. And don't forget to check your local event calendar for festivals, outdoor concerts, or markets. There's always something happening—you just need to look!

Put on your comfiest walking shoes, grab a map (or let Google Maps be your guide), and set off to rediscover *the charm of your own city.*

You'll see your hometown through fresh eyes and feel the thrill of adventure—without the hassle of packing or jet lag!

3. Explore Nature
The Great Outdoors Awaits

Nature is calling, and it's leaving a voicemail that says, „Get out here and enjoy the great outdoors!" There's nothing quite like spending time surrounded by nature's beauty—whether standing at the edge of a breathtaking canyon, hiking through a forest with the scent of pine in the air, or cruising along a scenic highway with the windows down and the music up.

> Reconnecting with nature
> isn't just good for the soul;
> it's a fantastic way to refresh
> your *mind, body, and spirit.*

Plus, it gives you the perfect excuse to finally wear that adventurous-looking hat you bought ages ago.

Now, planning a nature day trip doesn't have to be a grand expedition. Start small with a visit to a nearby park or nature reserve. Want to turn it up a notch? Map out a day trip to a national park or a scenic area you've always wanted to explore. Try a leisurely scenic drive if you want to dip your toes into the great outdoors without committing to an entire hike. There's something incredibly soothing about winding roads, stunning vistas, and the occasional roadside diner with the best pie in town.

A little preparation goes a long way for a successful day in nature. First, check the weather forecast—nothing ruins a nature day faster than a surprise downpour when you've forgotten your umbrella. Pack a small bag with essentials: water, snacks, a first-aid kit, bug spray and sunscreen. And don't forget your camera—nature is notoriously photogenic, and you'll want to capture those moments when you feel one with the earth.

And here's a tip from a particularly enthusiastic squirrel I met on a trail (let's call him Sir Nutty)—take your time. Nature isn't going anywhere, so there's no need to rush. Pause to listen to the birds, breathe in the fresh air, and soak in the scenery. If you're up for it, bring a journal or sketchbook and let the surroundings inspire you. You never know; the great outdoors might just unlock your inner poet—or at least give you something to brag about at your next dinner party.

4. Hit the Trails
The Joy of Hiking

Ready to lace up those boots and hit the trails? Hiking is nature's version of a roller coaster—minus the loops and the screaming (unless you see a snake, then scream away). It's the perfect way to explore the great outdoors, get some exercise, and maybe even discover that you're a lot more adventurous than you thought.

First things first, let's talk trails. If you're new to hiking, start with something gentle—a trail that offers scenic views without making you feel like you've accidentally signed up for a marathon. Look for local trails that are well-marked and rated as easy or moderate. Apps like AllTrails are a hiker's best friend, offering detailed trail maps, difficulty ratings, and even reviews from other hikers who've gone before you. Seasoned hiker? Challenge yourself with a more rugged path—perhaps something with a waterfall or a summit that gives you that „king of the world" feeling.

Now, safety isn't just for the cautious—it's for the smart. Before you head out, check the weather and trail conditions. Dress in layers because nature likes to play tricks with temperatures. Always pack the essentials: your cell phone, water, snacks, a map, a flashlight, sunscreen, bug spray, and a first-aid kit. If you're going solo, let someone know where you're headed. And if you're hiking in a group, keep an eye on each other—nothing bonds friends like getting lost in the woods and finding your way back together.

Speaking of trails, some spots are so popular they're practically nature's red carpet. Consider checking out places like the Appalachian Trail, the Pacific Crest Trail, or even local favorites like the Smoky Mountains or the Shenandoah National Park. These trails offer stunning views, varied terrains, and the kind of fresh air that makes you want to bottle it up and take it home.

Those who enjoy the social side of hiking should consider joining an organized hiking group. Local community centers, outdoor clubs, and online platforms like Meetup.com often host group hikes, giving you the chance to meet fellow nature lovers and explore new trails together.

It's a great way to stay motivated, make new friends, and share the joy of hiking with others.

Get your walking stick (or just a sturdy stick you find along the way) and hit the trails. With every step, you'll discover new sights, breathe in that crisp, clean air, and maybe even find yourself humming „The Hills Are Alive." Happy hiking, trailblazer!

5. Relive Your Youth
Adult Summer Camps

Who says summer camp is just for kids? Pack your bug spray and get ready to relive those carefree days of cabin life, minus the curfew, with a much better selection of snacks. Adult summer camps are the ultimate playground for retirees looking to dive into a world of fun, friendship, and maybe even a bit of arts and crafts—macaroni necklaces, anyone?

Picture this: You arrive at camp, and instead of a bunkmate who snores, you're paired with someone who knows how to make a mean margarita. Your days are filled with activities ranging from paddleboarding on the lake to pottery classes that might reveal your inner artist (or at least give you a good laugh when your pot looks more like a lumpy ashtray). Evenings are reserved for campfires, complete with s'mores and sing-alongs, where you can belt out classics without worrying about your kids rolling their eyes.

Finding the *perfect adult summer camp* is easier than roasting the perfect marshmallow.

Websites like Camp No Counselors and Club Getaway specialize in creating experiences catering to various interests. Whether you're looking to unleash your inner athlete with adventure sports, explore your creative side with art workshops, or simply relax with yoga by the lake, there's a camp for you. These camps are scattered across the country, so you can pick one close to home or turn it into a road trip to remember. Let me tell you about when I went to an adult summer camp and ended up in a talent show. My act? Reciting Shakespearean sonnets while juggling. It wasn't exactly Broadway-worthy, but I brought the house down (and nearly my juggling balls). The best part? The friends I made that week have become my go-to crew for all things fun. We even have a yearly camp reunion—no juggling required.

Why not trade in your TV remote for a canoe paddle and your slippers for some hiking boots? Adult summer camps offer an incredible mix of nostalgia and new experiences, proving that you're never too old to make new memories—or be a little silly while doing it. Sign up, pack up, and get ready for the best summer ever!

6. A New Home Base
Relocate to Affordable Retirement Havens

Ready to shake things up and find a new nest for your golden years without emptying your nest egg? Relocating to an affordable retirement haven might just be your next big adventure. It's like finding a cozy new spot where your dollars stretch further and the sun shines brighter. The neighbors are as friendly as the barista who knows your coffee order by heart.

Exploring affordable locations is like *hunting for hidden treasure.*

Places like Asheville, North Carolina, or Tucson, Arizona, offer a blend of great weather, vibrant communities, and lower costs of living. And let's not forget those international options—Portugal, anyone? With its stunning coastlines, delicious cuisine, and affordable healthcare, it's no wonder retirees are flocking there faster than you can say „pastel de nata.“

But doing a little homework is essential before you start packing those boxes. Start by making a list of what matters most to you: healthcare, climate, community activities, and, of course, the cost of living. Once you've got your priorities in order, dive into some research. Websites like BestPlaces or Numbeo can help you compare living costs and quality of life across different locations. Don't stop there—visit potential new homes in person to get a real feel for the area. Spend a few days exploring local markets, chatting with residents, and sampling the local cuisine (because food is life, after all).

And here's a little pro tip: Consider renting before you commit. This way, you can test the waters without diving in headfirst. It's like trying on a new pair of shoes—walking around the store a bit before taking them home is better.

7. Affordable Adventures
Top Budget-Friendly Travel Destinations

Are you ready to see the world without feeling like you've emptied your entire piggy bank? Let's take a detailed look into some amazing, wallet-friendly destinations that offer rich experiences and lifelong memories without making your budget cry for mercy.

PORTUGAL

———

Portugal is Europe's best-kept secret—until you discover it and wonder why everyone isn't already there. From Lisbon's charming streets to the Algarve's sunny beaches, you'll find a mix of culture, history, and stunning landscapes. And the best part? It's super affordable. Stay in a quaint guesthouse, savor delicious seafood (try the pastel de nata for dessert!), and use the excellent public transport to explore this beautiful country on a dime.

GREECE

———

Yes, Greece! But instead of the pricey tourist hubs, check out the Peloponnese region or the lesser-known islands like Naxos or Paros. You'll find crystal-clear waters, ancient ruins, and mouth-watering Greek cuisine at prices that won't require a financial bailout. Plus, the slower pace of life in these areas is perfect for soaking in the local culture without the crowds.

MEXICO

Skip the touristy spots and head to cities like Guanajuato or Oaxaca. These destinations are rich in culture, with vibrant markets, stunning colonial architecture, and mouth-watering street food at prices that won't make you sweat. You can enjoy an authentic Mexican experience, from sipping tequila with the locals to exploring ancient ruins without breaking the bank.

VIETNAM

If Southeast Asia has been calling your name, Vietnam should be at the top of your list. It's a feast for the senses—think bustling markets, serene beaches, and awe-inspiring natural wonders like Ha Long Bay. The cost of living here is incredibly low, so you can live like royalty on a backpacker's budget. Don't miss the street food in Hanoi; a bowl of pho will warm your heart without empty-ing your wallet.

Travel Hacks: Stretching Your Travel Dollar Even Further

Go Off-Season

Traveling during the shoulder season (just before or after peak season) can save you a bundle on flights and accommodations, and you'll avoid the tourist crush.

Stay Longer

Many places offer discounts for more extended stays. Opt for weekly or monthly rates on Airbnb or negotiate directly with local guesthouses.

Eat Local

Skip the fancy restaurants and dive into the local food scene. Street food and local eateries give you an authentic taste of the culture and keep your budget in check.

Walk or Bike

Explore on foot or by bike to save on transportation costs and see the sights up close. Many cities have bike rental programs or free walking tours—a double win for your budget and health!

8. Cultural Immersion
Attend Local Festivals and Events

Are you looking to spice up your retirement with a little bit of culture? Festivals, concerts, and theater performances are your golden ticket to diving headfirst into the vibrant heart of any destination. These events aren't just about watching from the sidelines—they're about dancing in the streets, tasting new foods, and discovering traditions that might just become your new favorite memories.

Firstly, let's talk about festivals. From the tomato-throwing madness of Spain's La Tomatina to the colorful, joyous chaos of India's Holi, festivals offer an immersive experience that go way beyond just entertainment. You'll find yourself surrounded by locals who are more than happy to share their traditions—and perhaps a few tips on avoiding getting splattered in tomato juice.

Now, how do you find these gems? Start by checking local tourism websites or apps like Eventbrite and Time Out, which list upcoming events by location. You can even set up alerts for specific types of events—never miss out on a jazz festival or a craft fair again! Another tip: Don't shy away from asking the locals. Sometimes, the best events are the ones that aren't plastered all over the Internet, and a quick chat with a local shopkeeper or barista might lead you to the most authentic cultural experience of your trip.

Planning your travels around these events is a breeze, too. Book your accommodations early once you've got your eye on an event—the festival season can fill up fast! And while you're at it, why not extend your stay a few days before or after the event? This gives you time to explore the area without the crowds and perhaps uncover an unsung wonder or two.

There is no better way to feel the pulse of a place than by joining in its celebrations—just remember to bring your dancing shoes and an appetite for adventure!

9. Travel Buddies
Join a Travel Group

Who says traveling solo is the only way to see the world? When you join a travel group, you are stepping into an adventure with a built-in crew of friends—perfect for those who love a bit of company on the road. The social benefits are endless: you can swap stories, share laughs, and maybe even snag some insider tips from seasoned travelers. Plus, there's something comforting about knowing someone's got your back if you forget your passport in the hotel room... again.

Group travel isn't just about camaraderie; it's also a fantastic way to *ensure your safety.*

With a group, you're less likely to find yourself lost in a foreign city or stranded without a taxi. There's safety in numbers, and travel groups often have local guides who know the ropes, making your journey smoother and stress-free.

Now, let's talk about finding your tribe. Travel clubs like Road Scholar or Meetup groups dedicated to travel are great starting points. These platforms connect you with people who share your wanderlust and might be looking for a new friend to explore with. And don't forget about specialty groups, too! There are clubs for solo travelers, foodies, history buffs—you name it. Joining a group aligned with your interests enhances your travel experience. It makes it easier to bond with your new travel buddies.

Speaking of bonding, let me tell you about my bestie, Karen. She decided to join a travel group on a whim, and now she's got a whole squad of pals from all over the world. On her last trip to Italy, she ended up sharing gelato with a couple from Australia, hiking with a retiree from New Zealand, and learning to make pasta from a chef in Tuscany. Karen returned with more than souvenirs—she gained lifelong friends and countless stories to tell.

So, why go it alone when you can have a whole crew of travel buddies to share the ride? Pack your bags, sign up for a group, and prepare for adventures that are twice as fun when experienced together!

10. Travel with a Purpose
Voluntourism Opportunities

Why just sightsee when you can make a difference? Voluntourism mixes the thrill of exploring new places with the heartwarming joy of giving back. Picture yourself teaching English in a small village, helping with wildlife conservation, or even building homes for communities in need. Not only do you get to immerse yourself in a new culture, but you also leave a positive mark on the places you visit. Plus, the stories you'll have to tell? Priceless.

Finding the right voluntourism opportunity is *easier than you'd think.*

Start with organizations like Globe Aware or Projects Abroad, which offer a wide range of volunteer programs tailored to your skills and passions. Love animals? Consider volunteering with WWF's Earth Hour or GoEco on wildlife conservation projects. More of a people person? Habitat for Humanity lets you roll up your sleeves and help build homes in communities worldwide. And for those who prefer something a little less hands-on, teaching or community support projects are always in demand.

To ensure your voluntourism experience is as impactful as it is enjoyable, make sure to research programs thoroughly. Look for organizations that are transparent about their goals, have a proven track record, and align with your values. A little prep work goes a long way in ensuring your efforts are meaningful to you and the community you're helping.

And here's a fun nugget—on a trip to Costa Rica, one traveler ended up painting a school with a group of locals. By the end of the week, they had a freshly painted school and a brand-new circle of friends who threw them a farewell party complete with traditional dancing and homemade tamales. Now, that's what you call a win-win adventure! So, grab your passport, pack your bags, and get ready to do some good in the world, one destination at a time.

ADVENTURE AWAITS

– YOUR NEXT GREAT JOURNEY STARTS NOW

So here you are, at the gateway to the world—no longer tied to a desk, a calendar full of meetings, or the 9-to-5 grind. Retirement isn't the end; it's the grand beginning of your next great adventure! Travel isn't just a way to pass the time; it's your golden ticket to a life filled with joy, discovery, and maybe even a few hilarious mishaps that'll make for great stories later on.

Remember, every journey you take is a chance to add a new chapter to your life's story. Whether hiking through lush forests, wandering through the streets of a new city, or sipping coffee at a local café halfway across the world, each experience will enrich your life and broaden your horizons.

You've worked hard, and now it's time to reap the rewards —*one exciting destination at a time.*

So, dust off that suitcase, pull out the map and start planning. The world is waiting for you, full of places to see, people to meet, and memories to make. Don't hesitate—pack your curiosity, sense of humor, and maybe an extra pair of socks. Your next adventure is just around the corner, and trust me, it will be one heck of a ride!

CHAPTER TEN

GIVING BACK

Volunteering and Community Involvement

Retirement is finally reaching the summit after a long, winding climb—you're at the top, the view is fantastic, and there's no rush to get back down. But once you're there, what's next? It turns out that one of the most fulfilling ways to enjoy this newfound freedom is by giving back to your community.

After all, you've spent decades gathering wisdom, skills, and experiences—why not *spread the wealth*?

Picture this: a retired neighbor of mine started volunteering at the local animal shelter. Now, he's the kind of guy who spent most of his career behind a desk, so the idea of wrangling puppies and kittens wasn't exactly on his radar. But he was the shelter's superstar within weeks—cooing over every critter and organizing adoption events like a pro. The best part? He found a whole new social circle of like-minded animal lovers and discovered a joy he never expected. Plus, he's never been happier.

Volunteering is all about finding a new sense of purpose, connecting with others, and having a good time while you're at it. Whether mentoring the next generation, organizing community events, or simply offering a helping hand, giving back in retirement can be the most rewarding adventure yet.

Enriching Your Life Through Volunteering

You know that warm, fuzzy feeling you get when you've done something kind? Volunteering gives you that but on turbo mode. Studies have shown that lending a hand can boost your mood, reduce stress, and even lower blood pressure. Who needs a prescription when you've got community service?

But the perks don't stop there. Volunteering is also the key to feeling connected and valued. Remember that sense of belonging you had back in the day, whether it was at work, in a club, or just with your old gang of friends? Volunteering can bring that back in a big way. You're not just a retiree - you're an important part of something bigger. Whether you're organizing a neighborhood cleanup or mentoring kids at the local school, you'll find yourself surrounded by people who share your passion and enthusiasm. There's nothing quite like swapping stories with your new buddies over a cup of coffee after a day of doing good.

In short, volunteering is like a multivitamin for your soul. It keeps you active, connected, and feeling absolutely fabulous.

The Ripple Effect
Impacting Your Community

When you toss a pebble into a pond, those ripples spread far and wide—just like your acts of kindness in the community. Every small effort you make has the power to spark positive change that can grow beyond what you'd ever expect. Think of it as the butterfly effect but with more high-fives and less chaos theory. Maybe you're planting flowers in a neglected park or helping out at the local food bank. Whatever it is, your contributions are the spark that can light up an entire neighborhood.

And here's the cherry on top: giving back doesn't just improve the community—it deepens your connections within it. Suddenly, the people you used to wave to from across the street are now your partners in crime (the good kind) in making the world a better place. You're sharing laughs, stories, and maybe even the secret to perfecting your grandmother's cookie recipe. Before you know it, you're part of a tightly-knit group of folks who care about where they live and each other.

Don't be afraid to be the pebble in the pond. Your efforts will not only beautify and improve your community but will also forge stronger relationships with those around you. And who knows? You might even start a chain reaction of kindness that keeps spreading.

Finding Purpose and Fulfillment

Who says retirement is about slowing down? It's the perfect time to kick things into high gear by putting all those years of skills and experience to good use. Volunteering is the encore performance of your career, but this time, you're calling the shots. Whether you've spent decades in an office, on the front lines, or running the show at home, there's a world of opportunities where your expertise can make a real difference. Imagine it as giving your talents a new stage to shine on—minus the performance reviews.

Now, let's talk about rediscovering those passions that may have taken a backseat during your working years. Volunteering is about reigniting the spark that makes you jump out of bed in the morning (or at least shuffle over to the coffee pot with a bit more enthusiasm). Maybe you've always had a soft spot for animals or secretly wanted to mentor the next generation of budding entrepreneurs. Volunteering lets you dive back into those interests, turning your free time into fulfilling, passion-driven adventures.

Overcoming Your Fears

Let's discuss those nagging doubts that can pop up when you think about volunteering. It's easy to have doubts and ask, „What do I have to offer?" But trust me, everyone has something valuable to contribute—even if it's just the ability to whip up a mean batch of cookies for the bake sale. Years ago, when he retired, my uncle was convinced he didn't have much to offer after spending most of his life working in accounting. He didn't realize that his knack for numbers was exactly what the local community center needed to balance their books. Now, he's practically a legend there—legendary for keeping the budget in check and for his impromptu math jokes. The point is that your skills, no matter how mundane they might seem to you, can be a real game-changer for others.

Now, about that fear of commitment—retirement is supposed to be about freedom, right? The last thing you want is to feel like you've signed up for something that will consume your time. Here's the trick: start small. Dip your toes in with a one-off event or a short-term project. You don't have to jump in with both feet right away. Think of it as trying out a new hobby—if you like it, you can always do more. If it's not your cup of tea, no harm done. Volunteering is all about finding what works for you on your terms. And who knows? You might just find that a little bit of commitment goes a long way in bringing a lot of joy and satisfaction into your life.

Practical Tips to Make Volunteering a Fun Adventure

Volunteering should be as enjoyable and fulfilling as it is beneficial to the community. Here's how you can jump into the world of giving back without feeling overwhelmed.

Finding Volunteer Opportunities:

Websites like VolunteerMatch, Idealist, and local community boards are filled with volunteering opportunities. You can filter by your interests and availability to find a cause that sparks your passion. Don't overlook local nonprofits, religious groups, or community centers either—sometimes, the best opportunities are just around the corner. Pop by your neighborhood church, synagogue, or mosque, or stroll to your local library to discover where your help might be most needed.

Balancing Volunteering and Leisure:

Volunteering should never feel like a chore. To keep it light and enjoyable, set clear time limits for your commitments and blend them seamlessly with your leisure activities. Whether it's dedicating an hour a week or a few days a month, decide what works best for you and stick to it. Schedule your volunteering around your favorite activities—this ensures you're giving back while enjoying your retirement to the fullest.

Networks and Resources for Support:

Connect with fellow volunteers to share experiences, ideas, and support through local volunteer groups or online communities. Don't forget to tap into your local library, senior center, or online forums for volunteering ideas and connections. These resources often host events or have bulletin boards with information on where help is needed, making it easier to meet like-minded folks who share your enthusiasm for giving back.

Getting Started: First Steps in Volunteering.

Reflect on what makes you tick and match your volunteer work with your interests to make the experience enjoyable. Love gardening? Perhaps a community garden needs your green thumb. Passionate about education? Maybe mentoring could be your niche. Start with short-term or low-commitment opportunities to ease into volunteering. Try a weekend event or a one-time project to see how it fits into your life. If you enjoy it, you can always expand your role—starting small keeps things manageable and fun!

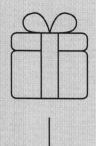

EXCITING WAYS TO GIVE BACK!

Next, I will share with you some fun and fulfilling ways to give back to your community. From volunteering at local shelters to mentoring the next generation, there are countless ways to make a positive impact. And the best part? Each activity is not just about giving; it's also about connecting, learning, and growing.

1. Volunteer in Your Community

Ready to roll up your sleeves and dive into some community goodness? Let's start with local shelters and environmental projects.

Whether serving meals at a food bank or joining a beach cleanup crew, there's *no shortage of ways* to make a meaningful difference.

As an added benefit, you'll meet some incredible people along the way—fellow do-gooders who might just become your new best friends.

But wait, there's more! Schools and libraries are always on the lookout for folks with a bit of time and a lot of heart. You could tutor students, help organize events, or even just lend a hand with book sorting at your local library. It's a great way to share your wisdom (and maybe show off those stellar math skills) while supporting the next generation.

2. Mentoring

Have you ever thought about sharing all that wisdom you've gathered over the years?

Mentoring helps
the next generation
shine even brighter.

Whether it's guiding a young whippersnapper through the maze of life or offering a peer some friendly advice, mentoring is a fantastic way to stay connected and make a meaningful impact.

Getting started is a breeze. You can look into mentoring programs like Big Brothers Big Sisters, where you can team up with a younger person who could use a little guidance and a lot of encouragement. Or, if you've got a soft spot for education, local schools are always on the lookout for mentors to help students navigate their academic and personal journeys. It's a win-win situation—you get to flex those brain muscles, and they get a boost of confidence and wisdom. Plus, you might just pick up a few new tricks yourself!

3. Babysitting

Who says babysitting is just for teenagers looking to make a few bucks?

Offering your time to babysit for busy parents is a brilliant way to *give back* while *staying connected* with the younger generation.

It's a lot of fun—think of it as your personal ticket to relive the joy of building pillow forts, making silly faces, and discovering the latest (and sometimes baffling) kids' trends. Not to mention, you'll be a hero to those parents who could use a night out or a quiet afternoon to themselves.

So, how do you enter into the wonderful world of babysitting? Start by spreading the word among your neighbors, friends, and local community groups that you're available to help. If you're tech-savvy, you can even join local Facebook groups where families often post babysitting requests. Libraries and community centers are also great places to connect with families who might need an extra pair of hands.

And let's be honest—there's something truly heartwarming about being the go-to babysitter. You'll build lasting relationships with these little ones, become the trusted adult they look forward to seeing, and hey, you might even earn a reputation as the coolest babysitter in town! The best part is you get to hand them back at the end of the day and take a well-deserved break! So grab those storybooks and snack supplies, and get ready to be the delightful, dependable, and downright fun babysitter every family wishes they had.

4. Take Care of Your Grandchildren

Spending time with grandchildren is like getting a backstage pass to the best show in town—a heartwarming, laughter-filled adventure that's on repeat! There's nothing quite like the joy of watching little ones grow, sharing your wisdom (and maybe a few secret cookie recipes), and building memories that'll be cherished for a lifetime. Whether helping with homework, going on spontaneous park adventures, or simply being there for a chat, the bond you create with your grandkids is priceless.

But what if your grandkids are far away, or you want to spread grandparent love beyond your own family? That's where becoming a substitute grandparent comes in. Programs like Foster Grandparents connect you with families who could use a little extra support, offering you the chance to step into the role of an honorary grandparent. It's a beautiful way to make a difference in a child's life and to fill your days with the warmth and joy that only comes from being the wise, caring, and slightly mischievous grandparent figure every kid dreams of.

Embrace the role of the *fun-loving, cookie-baking, story-sharing grandparent*—whether it's with your own grandkids or as a substitute for a family in need.

It's a win-win for everyone involved, and your heart will be fuller than a cookie jar at grandma's house!

5. Declutter and Donate

Let's talk about decluttering—aka, finding your long-lost floor under that mountain of „stuff" that's been growing for decades. Not only will clearing out your home make it feel like you've gained a few hundred square feet, but it also gives you the chance to make someone else's day by donating those forgotten treasures.

First, tackle those closets, attics, and basements where everything from old ski boots to Grandma's questionable vase collection has been collecting dust. Sorting through it all can feel like a treasure hunt—just with a lot more sneezing. Think of it this way - as you simplify your life, you're giving those once-loved items a new lease on life in someone else's home.

So, where do you send your bounty of decluttered goods? Thrift stores like Goodwill and Salvation Army are classic choices, where your donations can help fund job training and other community programs. If you've got gently-used clothes, consider local shelters that are always in need. And for those unique or quirky items, online platforms like Freecycle or Facebook Marketplace can connect you with folks who will appreciate your once-loved treasures.

Decluttering is about so much more than just clearing out your space. It's a chance to *share the joy* and *lighten someone else's load,* too.

Crawl into that storage space, and watch the good karma roll in as you donate those forgotten goodies to those who could use them. It's got all of the fun of a yard sale—minus the haggling!

6. Support Charitable Projects

Let's get real: giving back doesn't have to mean emptying your wallet—it can also mean rolling up your sleeves and donating some good old-fashioned elbow grease. If you've got time to spare, why not volunteer for a fundraising event? Maybe you're a whiz with numbers, or you can organize a closet like a pro. Charities always need skills like accounting, marketing, or simply keeping everything running smoothly.

> ## Your talents could be the secret that takes a good cause from „*meh*" to „*wow!*"

But if your time is already booked solid—or you're just not ready to trade retirement for yet another calendar full of commitments—making a financial contribution is another powerful way to make a difference. When donating money, a little research goes a long way. Look for charities that align with your passions, and check out their financials to make sure your hard-earned dollars are being put to good use. Websites like Charity Navigator or GuideStar can help you find trustworthy organizations where your donation will have the most significant impact.

Whether giving your time, skills, or money, you're making the world a better place. And nothing feels better than knowing you're spreading a little joy and making a real difference.

7. Neighborhood Initiatives

If you've ever dreamed of turning your neighborhood into a vibrant, close-knit community, now's your chance to roll up your sleeves and make it happen. Community gardens and block parties are two fantastic ways to dive in, get involved, and maybe even become the local legend who brought everyone together!

Let's start with community gardens. These little green havens are perfect for sprouting friendships along with your veggies. You don't need to be a gardening guru to get started—just a willingness to dig in and share a laugh or two with your neighbors. Whether you're planting tomatoes, herbs, or a mystery plant that someone swears is zucchini, you're not just growing food—you're cultivating a sense of togetherness. Plus, it's a great excuse to trade gardening tips, share homegrown produce, and maybe even host a „Who Grew the Biggest Pumpkin" contest.

And let's not forget about block parties—the social glue that can turn a street of strangers into a squad of friends. Organizing a block party doesn't have to be complicated. Start with the basics: some food, music, and a few lawn chairs. Toss in a barbecue, a potluck, or even a theme (Hawaiian luau, anyone?), and you've got yourself a recipe for community magic. Block parties are a chance to bond, laugh, and share stories with the folks you see daily but rarely get to know. The added bonus? You're strengthening the fabric of your community, creating a safer, friendlier place for everyone.

8. Host a Charity Event

Hosting a charity event is a great way to make a difference while having a blast. Whether it's whipping up cupcakes for a bake sale, getting your steps in with a walk-a-thon, or turning your clutter into cash with a charity yard sale, there's no shortage of ways to rally your community for a cause you care about.

First things first—choose your event. Bake sales are always a hit (who can resist homemade cookies?), but if you want to stretch those legs, a walk-a-thon could be your ticket to success. Feeling ambitious? A silent auction can turn your neighbors into fierce bidders, all for a good cause. Or, if you're staring down a garage full of „treasures" you're ready to part with, why not host a charity yard sale? It's a win-win: you declutter, and the proceeds go to a cause that makes your heart happy.

Now, let's talk strategy. The key to a successful event is getting your community on board. Start by spreading the word like wildfire—post on local social media groups, send out flyers and don't underestimate the power of word-of-mouth. You might even convince that one neighbor who never leaves their house to show up and chip in! Consider creating a catchy hashtag for the event, something like #BakeForGood or #WalkWithPurpose, to boost your cause online.

Make sure there's plenty of cheer and excitement on the big day. Set up a donation jar for those who can't resist giving a little extra and have some fun activities or games to keep everyone entertained. And don't forget the power of a great story—share the impact your event will have on the chosen charity to inspire even more generosity.

By the end of the day, you'll have raised funds, strengthened your community, and maybe even discovered a hidden talent for auctioneering. Who knew making a difference could be this much fun?

9. Become a Pen Pal to Those in Need

Who doesn't love a good old-fashioned letter? There's something wonderfully heartwarming about receiving a handwritten note in a world of instant messages and emojis. Now, imagine the joy of someone in need opening a letter filled with kind words and cheerful thoughts. That's where you come in—the pen pal who brightens someone's day.

> Writing letters to isolated individuals, like seniors in nursing homes or those who are incarcerated, is a simple yet powerful way to *spread kindness* and *make meaningful connections.*

You might be surprised how much a thoughtful note can lift someone's spirits, offering a connection to the outside world and a reminder that they're not forgotten. Additionally, you get the joy of knowing you've made a difference without even leaving your cozy chair—how's that for a win-win?

If you're wondering where to start, there are fantastic programs out there that make it easy to get involved. Letters Against Isolation is one such organization that connects volunteers with lonely seniors who would love to receive some friendly correspondence. They'll guide you on what to write and even match you with someone in need. If you're interested in writing to incarcerated individuals, organizations like WriteAPrisoner.com can help you find a pen pal who can use uplifting words.

So grab your favorite pen, pick out some cheerful stationery, and get ready to share a bit of your world with someone who could use a friend. You just never know—you might make a lifelong connection and become someone's favorite pen pal!

10. Advocacy and Activism

Do you want to channel that inner fire and make a difference? Advocacy and activism are your tickets to turning passion into action. Whether it's championing environmental conservation, fighting for social justice, or pushing for policy changes, getting involved in advocacy lets you stand up for what you believe in—and have some fun doing it!

First, pick a cause that really gets you excited. Maybe you're passionate about protecting the planet, advocating for equal rights, or ensuring everyone can access quality healthcare. Whatever it is, there's a movement out there that could use your voice, energy, and enthusiasm.

Now, let's talk about how to get involved. Start by looking for local advocacy groups or national organizations that align with your cause. Groups like the Sierra Club are fantastic for those interested in environmental issues. At the same time, Amnesty International is an excellent choice if you're passionate about human rights. These organizations often have local chapters, making connecting with like-minded individuals and getting started in your community effortless.

Feeling bold? You could also join or support grassroots movements—those are the ones that often start small but pack a punch. Sign petitions, participate in rallies, write to your representatives, or volunteer your time to help organize events.

The key is to stay informed, stay involved, and *keep that passion burning bright.*

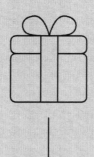

THE POWER OF GIVING BACK

As you've seen throughout this chapter, giving back in retirement is like adding a joyful rhythm to your days, bringing purpose, connection, and a dash of adventure into your life. Whether you're volunteering at a local shelter, mentoring the next generation, or hosting a lively charity event, every act of kindness makes a ripple in the world around you. And let's not forget—you're not just contributing to your community; you're enriching your own life in ways that bring happiness and fulfillment.

Stepping into these roles may seem like a small gesture, but the impact is enormous.

It's about staying busy
while creating a legacy
of *compassion and connection.*

So go ahead, embrace the opportunities to give back, laugh a little louder, and make every moment count. Your retirement years are your time to shine, and there's no better way to do that than by making a difference, one meaningful act at a time.

CHEERS TO RETIREMENT: YOUR NEXT GREAT JOURNEY

Congratulations!

You've made it through this entire guide, which means you're now armed with all the wisdom, tips, and a few good laughs to make your retirement years nothing short of spectacular. As you stand on the brink of this exciting new chapter, let's take a moment to celebrate the journey ahead—one filled with joy, purpose and a whole lot of adventure.

Now, let me tell you about Lesley. Lesley had always been a bit of a night owl, fascinated by the stars. But with the hustle and bustle of work and life, her love for stargazing had always taken a back seat. That changed the moment she retired. Lesley decided to dust off her old telescope, which she bought years ago and never got around to using. Before long, she wasn't just peering at the stars from her backyard; she joined a local astronomy club.

Lesley started attending star parties—those are gatherings where fellow sky enthusiasts set up their telescopes in open fields, far from the city lights, to gaze at the wonders of the universe. One chilly night, she spotted Saturn's rings for the first time, and it was like the universe had handed her a front-row seat to its greatest show. She was hooked. Soon, Lesley was the go-to person in her club for all things celestial. She even started hosting stargazing nights, inviting friends and neighbors to share in the awe of the night sky.

But it wasn't just about the stars but about rekindling and sharing a passion with others. Lesley's journey didn't just bring her closer to the cosmos; it brought her closer to her community, creating connections as deep as the night sky she loved to explore.

That's the magic of retirement. It's not about slowing down but finding new ways to speed up, laugh louder, and love deeper. It's a time to rediscover the things that make your heart sing, whether traveling to far-off places, volunteering in your community, or exploring the mysteries of the universe from your own backyard. This is your chance to write the best chapters of your life, full of the things that bring you joy and fulfillment.

And if there's one thing I want you to take away from this book, it's this: Retirement is your time to shine. It's not the end of the road; it's an entirely new journey with endless possibilities and a world of experiences waiting for you. So embrace each day with a smile, try something new, give back to others, and never stop exploring.

Here's to the next adventure —*your best one yet.*

The road is wide open, the possibilities are endless, and the best part? You're in the driver's seat, ready to steer your life in any direction you choose. Buckle up, grab a friend, and enjoy the ride. Your most incredible adventure is just beginning!

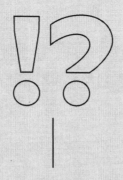

THANK YOU FOR JOINING US ON THIS JOURNEY!

We hope this book brought you inspiration, fun, and new ideas for making the most of retirement.
If you enjoyed it, we would be incredibly grateful if you could **leave a review on Amazon**—it means a lot to us and helps other readers discover the book.
We're always looking to improve, so if you have any suggestions or feedback, **simply scan this QR code to share your thoughts with us.**

THANK YOU AGAIN, AND HERE'S TO A FULFILLING AND EXCITING RE-TIREMENT!

MORE FROM
TG EDITION

The Easiest Anti-Inflammatory Cookbook for Beginners -
Restore Your Health and Relieve Persistent Pain with Simple Recipes

Cozy Christmas Word Search for Adults:
Large Print Word Puzzles for Holiday Relaxation and Stress Relief